REGIONAL RESEARCH
COOPERATION

Work Group at the Fifth Workers' Conference, Regional Land Tenure Research Project, Fayetteville, Arkansas, December, 1945. A corner of the Project bulletin library shows at the right. One of the numerous regional maps in the conference room hangs on the wall in the rear. The 5 x 8 box on the table is the *Explanation of Codes* file. Average total attendance at each of the six workers' conferences was fourteen, and the average length of the conference was five days, the longest being ten days and the shortest, three days.

REGIONAL
RESEARCH COOPERATION

A Statement of Regional Research Procedures

as developed by

The Regional Land Tenure Research Project

B Y

Harold Hoffsommer

CHAPEL HILL

The University of North Carolina Press

PREFACE

The Regional Land Tenure Research Project, sponsored by the Southwestern Land Tenure Research Committee,* was made possible by the cooperation of the Agricultural Colleges of the five states of Arkansas, Louisiana, Mississippi, Oklahoma, and Texas. It had financial support from the General Education Board and the Farm Foundation and some additional aid in personnel and equipment from the United States Department of Agriculture.

The actual work of the Project began in the summer of 1942 at which time the regional office was established and the regional staff assembled. War conditions greatly retarded the work. As a result the original three-year term of duration was extended to four years. At the end of this period the Regional Office, according to plan, was disbanded. The materials collected, however, remain intact and are available and will doubtless continue to be worked on for some time to come, particularly in the individual states.

In view of the primacy of the undertaking in its particular sphere and its pertinence to all types of endeavor in the rapidly growing field of regional research, the experience of the Project is reported in some detail. Every attempt is made to give an objective picture with equal emphasis to its strong and weak points. The Project cooperators feel that they would be remiss in their obligation to the development of better scientific research methods if the full experience of the Project were not made available.

The writer has been associated with the Project during its entire period of operation, first as a member of the Southwestern Land Tenure Research Committee and then as Project Director when the Project was formally organized under the sponsorship of the Committee as the Regional Land Tenure Research Project. The account herewith presented is in the nature of a case study. Liberal use is made throughout of various reports of project procedure accumulated as the Project progressed. It is hoped that this account may constitute a partial guide to those undertaking regional research or, failing that, that it may at least serve to point out some of the crucial problems which are likely to be encountered in such research.

*C. O. Brannen, Chairman, University of Arkansas; Joseph Ackerman, Executive Secretary, Farm Foundation; O. D. Duncan, Oklahoma Agricultural and Mechanical College; Lippert Ellis, Bureau of Agricultural Economics; L. P. Gabbard, Texas Agricultural and Mechanical College; B. M. Gile, Louisiana State University; Peter Nelson, Oklahoma Agricultural and Mechanical College; Frank J. Welch, Mississippi State College.

Many people have aided in the preparation of this report. The author is especially indebted to Joseph Ackerman of the Farm Foundation for stimulation and encouragement throughout the Project and for his many valuable suggestions growing out of a nation-wide experience in matters of regional research organization.

Harold Hoffsommer

College Park, Maryland
November 18, 1947

CONTENTS

CONTENTS

CONTENTS

REGIONAL RESEARCH
COOPERATION

CHAPTER ONE

Objectives of the Regional Research Project

Stated briefly, the Regional Land Tenure Research Project had a two-fold purpose: (1) to study the subject of land tenure[1] in the five-state region[2] and (2) to develop a plan for regional research cooperation—which is the subject of this report.

The major objective of the study of land tenure was to relate farm tenure status to farm family social and economic performance. Carried forward on a regional level the study was designed: (1) to study cooperatively in the region the aspects of land tenure as indicated above, (2) to coordinate land tenure studies in the respective states so that their efforts would be complementary, (3) to provide direction and technical assistance so that the work in the several states would be more effective and their funds used

1. Both regional and state reports are in process from this aspect of the Project. The major regional subject matter report is being published by the University of North Carolina Press, Chapel Hill, N. C. under the title, *Social and Economic Significance of Land Tenure in the Southwestern States.* This report will comprise a sizeable volume, written by nine members of the regional organization. As Project Director, the writer edited this volume and prepared several of the chapters including the summary chapter which has been pre-printed for wider distribution under the title *Land Tenure in the Southwestern States, A Summary of Significant Findings of the Regional Land Tenure Research Project,* Southwestern Regional Bulletin No. 1, Agricultural Experiment Station Bulletin No. 482, University of Arkansas College of Agriculture, Fayetteville, Arkansas, October, 1948. State and other reports are listed in the Appendix.

2. The states included are Arkansas, Louisiana, Mississippi, Oklahoma, and Texas. The Regional Committee, known as the Southwestern Land Tenure Research Committee, did not include representatives from Mississippi until this Project was formed. Usually used in conjunction with the names of the cooperating states the project is referred to simply as the Regional Land Tenure Research Project, without designation of a specific region.

Throughout the writing of the regional report, the regional tenure workers referred to this group of states as the South Central Region. This designation was changed, however, by action of the Regional Committee just prior to publication of the report and was made to conform to the title of the Committee.

more efficiently, (4) to bring together materials on land tenure from the states in the region for use in a regional report that would deal primarily with some of the over-all aspects of land tenure, (5) to deal with the activities and implications of government programs and other institutional aspects of land tenure that could not, for various reasons, be dealt with as effectively by the individual states.

The second objective of the project, to develop a plan for regional research cooperation, is the chief concern of this report. What are the objectives of such a plan and why should it be developed? Among other purposes of the undertaking the following have been indicated by members of the Regional Committee and others:

1. Since modern transportation has greatly expanded the functioning areas of social and economic life, it is incumbent upon research workers to keep abreast of this development by working out new techniques and procedures applicable to these broader areas.

2. To measure the extent to which given problems are similar in scope and intensity from state to state throughout the area. That is, to measure the element of "commonality."

3. To utilize the advantage of approaching problems in concerted effort so that the scientific findings will have greater validity and recommendations made from such effort will have a broader base for legislative and other social action.

4. To stimulate local groups by letting them know that groups in a large area are giving thought to the same problems with which they are concerned.

5. To achieve the benefit to be gained in the association of thought and effort between the research workers of the various states and those spending their time purely on the regional effort.

6. To expand individual state research efforts.

7. Regional cooperative research has been talked about for many years. It is time that this approach be seriously tested out in order to verify its value, if any.

8. The regional approach gives a better opportunity for the

fusion of the several subject matter fields which are needed to study many problems. While these subject matter viewpoints might well be represented in a single state institution, their synthesis becomes more feasible when several states cooperate.

9. Finally, following a general trend of thought, government agencies and others are increasingly granting funds, the use of which are restricted to regional undertakings. It is therefore incumbent upon social researchers to develop techniques in this field.

TYPES OF REGIONAL RESEARCH

In regional work two broad types of collaborative effort between states may be distinguished: (1) cooperative research (2) coordinated research. The chief basis of distinction between these two types relates to the closeness with which the states collaborate in carrying forward the work. To be sure, in all types of regional research a minimum of cooperation of one kind or another is necessary. However, the term *cooperative research* as herein used is reserved for those situations in which the research procedures and activities are not only harmonious and coordinated as between the groups in question, but the labors are actually carried forward by joint action.

Both types assume a common regional problem but beyond that the procedure varies. *Cooperative* research presumes the collection of uniform data throughout the region. It also contemplates that the research workers of the region will work directly with one another in the tabulation and analysis of these data. This procedure necessitates careful organization and close cooperation but has several marked advantages. Among other things, it facilitates a concentrated attack on a common problem and at the same time makes possible a maximum of mutual helpfulness between the workers of the region in the collection, tabulation, and analysis of the research materials. In certain types of research it is probable that close similarity of work in several states might result in unnecessary repetition and duplication. The present lack of detailed knowledge and the wide diversity of conditions existing over any given region make it improbable, at least in the social sciences for some time to come, that this would prove a hindrance rather than a help.

In *coordinated* research the background problem is also common to the region, but here the research procedures in the several states need not be uniform nor are they necessarily addressed to identical phases of the problem. Rather the reliance for regional materials is placed upon the coordination of the state efforts so as to make their contributions complement and supplement each other. While this method lacks the strong element of commonality which makes possible detailed collaboration between the states on research techniques, and likewise close comparison of results, it has the advantage of giving a greater degree of freedom to each state both as to the selection of the specific problem of research emphasis and as to the techniques with which it will proceed. Also, since the collaboration is less closely knit than in cooperative research, the organization to carry it on can be somewhat less detailed. For example, in cooperative research, terms must be used identically throughout the region since detailed comparison of state data is one of the aims of this type of effort. Fewer organizational elements are needed where the aim of the effort does not include, as in coordinated research, comparisons of detailed data between the states.

The particular emphasis in the present project is on cooperative rather than coordinated research. The project plan carries with it not only the idea of working on a common problem throughout the region but of working together on this problem, using similar techniques and each worker aiding the other in the development of more efficient techniques.

The organization of the Project was such that it facilitated and amplified the work of the individual state experiment stations, and at the same time developed a pooling of effort which resulted in a regional product. Thus, the same basic data became the materials out of which both the state and regional reports were written. In addition, this approach has brought together several subject matter fields which bear upon the problem in question, which it would be less feasible to bring into cooperation if the study were conducted on a smaller area scale.

Summarized in a recent article concerning this project, the objective is stated thus:

"Social scientists have long discussed the feasibility of a regional approach to the study of economic and social problems but they have not as yet decisively advanced from the area of discussion to that of action. The Regional Project is an attempt to achieve this advance. It is true that valuable techniques have been developed for delineating regions and analyzing their contents, but little has been accomplished in bringing the social scientists of a given region together in such a way as to pool their interests and efforts on their common problems."[3]

As the Project progressed it became increasingly evident that the subject matter and the regional research plan objectives were very closely allied. A regional contribution to tenure research was found to be dependent, to a considerable extent, on an effective regional organization. Likewise, regional cooperation cannot operate in a vacuum. An effective research plan needs to be worked out on the basis of a real, not a hypothetical, subject matter problem. The former has at least the possibility of developing a workable plan of cooperation, whereas the most that could come from the latter would be speculation.

3. Harold Hoffsommer, "Organization and Objectives of the Regional Land Tenure Research Project," *Journal of Farm Economics*, XXV (February, 1943), 245.

CHAPTER TWO

Project Working Plan

PROJECT ORGANIZATION

The entire Project was under the sponsorship of a Regional Committee, which was made up of the heads of the departments of Agricultural Economics and Rural Sociology in the five state Agricultural Colleges, plus a representative from the Division of Land Economics, U. S. Department of Agriculture. In three of the states, since the departments of economics and sociology were combined under one head, one person represented both departments. In the remaining two states both a sociologist and an economist served on the committee.

Something of the history of the Project organization is set forth in the following quotation, written shortly after the project got under way.

"An adequate history of the Project cannot be set forth within the span of this brief report. Although its development has had its greatest growth in meetings held in 1941-1942, its roots go back a number of years to meetings of the Southwestern Social Science Association and the 'Outlook' meetings held in Texarkana. The committee personnel in at least three of the cooperating states has been constant over a period of years and although their group interests have not been consistently that of land tenure, they have formed the nucleus of a working relationship through long personal and professional acquaintance which is basic to an understanding of the present project growth.

"One of the earlier conferences which contributed directly to the formulation of the present Project was sponsored by the Farm Foundation and held in Texarkana in December, 1939.

"Two other groups, the Outlook Conference and the cooperators on the Bureau of Agricultural Economics Tenure Area Study, were meeting in Texarkana the same week. As a result of this arrangement of meetings nearly all of those in the area professionally interested in tenure study were brought together during this week.

"A follow-up of this meeting was called at Dallas in March, 1940 for the general purpose of coordinating the tenure work in the Southwestern states. This meeting was composed of the heads of the departments of Agricultural Economics in the states of Arkansas, Texas, Oklahoma, and Louisiana. The Southwestern Land Tenure Research Committee was formally organized at this time and decided on the broad subject matter approach of associating 'performance' with type of tenure.

"However long the regional idea had been harbored in the minds of individual members of the committee an important advancement on the regional front as a forerunner to the present study came at a meeting in St. Louis in February, 1941. This nation-wide meeting, sponsored by the Farm Foundation and the Bureau of Agricultural Economics through the North Central Regional Land Tenure Committee and the Southwestern Land Tenure Research Committee, included, among others, representatives from those states cooperating with the Bureau of Agricultural Economics Tenure Area Study. As the meeting progressed its members divided into sections representative of areas for the purpose of discussing the development of coordinate lines of tenure research within the several areas. The Southern group centered on two lines of approach: (1) tenure change, (2) the impact of government programs on tenure. No conclusive decisions were reached. However, following this meeting a small group representative of the Southwestern states met and formulated a general plan for that area.

"From this time on the Committee became quite active in the formulation of its program. In August, 1941 it met in Little Rock at which time the membership was broadened to include a rural sociologist from each of the two Experiment Stations in the area having such departments, also a representative from the Regional Office of the Bureau of Agricultural Economics. The Committee Chairman took the initiative in rounding up all state tenure materials including publications, lists of unpublished data, and plans for future tenure work. Against this background the Committee members, together with the Chairman, worked out proposed budgets and procedures of work for their individual states. These plans were then combined and approved by the Committee as a whole with the view of making a regional tenure study aided by funds from the Foundations.

"In January, 1942 the Committee again met in St. Louis with representatives of both the General Education Board and Farm Foundation in attendance to give the proposed project a hearing. Subsequently a meeting for further refinement of plans and procedures was held in Little Rock. Following the granting of funds by the Foundations the Committee met in Fayetteville and continues to have meetings at convenient points from time to time as the study progresses. Since the Committee is the final arbiter in all matters concerning the Project the agenda of these meetings cover a wide scope including budgetary matters, personnel, and the general subject matter content of the Project."[1]

The Regional Project was originally financed by a grant of $150,000 from the General Education Board and a somewhat smaller grant from the Farm Foundation. In order to secure these grants and to carry on the proposed cooperative activities of the Project each of the five states pledged varying amounts of personnel and traveling funds, according to the activities contemplated. In addition to this, the Bureau of Agricultural Economics, since it was already cooperating on tenure projects in all of the states, budgeted a sizable amount for cooperation with the Project. As the three-year period for which the Project was originally contemplated came to a close, it was evident that because of the emergency conditions existing during the project period, an extension of time would be needed. Consequently, the Project was extended and an additional $20,000 was granted by the General Education Board and certain additional funds made available by the Farm Foundation. In all, the assets of the Project, including the amounts budgeted by the states for personnel for the four-year period of its duration, amounted to somewhat over $375,000. In addition, before the original funds were granted, the Farm Foundation greatly aided in the formation of the project proposed by financing meetings and by giving the support of its own personnel.

Although the rather substantial grants from the out-of-state sources greatly facilitated the progress of the Project it should not be concluded that regional research is dependent on out-of-state

1. Harold Hoffsommer, "Organization and Objectives of the Regional Land Tenure Research Project," *Journal of Farm Economics*, XXV (February 1943), 246-48.

funds. The work of this project would obviously have been modified had it had available a less generous amount of outside funds, but it is believed that much the same techniques could have been used with a considerably smaller amount of outside support. In fact, with a moderate amount of funds available for regional purposes in each of the Experiment Stations, a project of this type could well be carried forward successfully. It should be borne in mind that a substantial part of the funds granted to this project were allotted for the specific purpose of experimental techniques in regional research. With the knowledge now at hand, it is believed that a similar project could be conducted with a considerable saving of both effort and expense.

After the funds were granted, one of the first problems faced by the Committee concerned the location of a regional headquarters. Chief considerations in the selection were suitable geographic location, availability of adequate physical plant, and the establishing of business relations for handling the funds. Early in the Committee discussions, it was decided that it would be most satisfactory to have one or the other of the cooperating institutions handle the funds, thus avoiding incorporation of the committee or payment of fees to an outside agency for disbursing the funds. After contacting the college business offices and assessing the pertinent situations in the several states the University of Arkansas was designated by the Committee as the disbursing agency for the Project. The Project paid the University a nominal monthly fee for this service.

The Committee felt that, although not mandatory, it was desirable that the physical headquarters be at the same place as the disbursing agency. Since the University of Arkansas was able and willing to make the larger part of a building available to the Project it was decided that the Project headquarters should also be located at the University of Arkansas. The demand for a central location with good transportation facilities could not be met entirely satisfactorily by any one of the five Experiment Stations in the region.

Having chosen the regional headquarters, a next important step was that of choosing a regional director and regional staff. The director was chosen from among the Regional Committee. He was then given the major responsibility in developing a regional staff.

Those on the payroll of the Regional Office were divided into four groups: (1) Director and central regional staff. The number on the central staff varied during the four-year project. The essential plan, however, included the employment of a statistician and one subject matter specialist for each of the three major fields concerned in the Project; that is, land economics, farm management, and rural sociology. In addition to the professional staff members there was a varying number of secretarial, clerical, and statistical workers. (2) Field Survey personnel. These constituted subject matter men attached to the central staff but assigned almost entirely to the states during the schedule-taking period of the Project. The Project had an average of four employees of this type during this period of its work. (3) Regional State Employees. These were the schedule takers hired for a period of six months or more. They were appointed by the Project Director on the recommendation of individual committee members for work mainly in the state in question. (4) Temporary Field Workers. These workers had essentially the same functions as the regional state employees, the chief difference being that their employment was somewhat more temporary.

As already stated, the Regional Committee sponsored the Project. Each committee member headed the work in his state. He was the project leader unless he turned over this function to someone else. The states varied in organization at this point from that where the head of the department (the committee member) was entirely responsible for the detailed conduct of the Project within his state to an arrangement whereby essentially the whole collaboration on the Project was turned over to a member of the department.

The Committee determined that any regional employee, while working in a given state, was to be under the direct supervision of the project leader in the state in which he was working. The state project leader was thus responsible for the accurate collection of the intensive survey data within his state, and regional employees when working in individual states were to have the same status as state department members. Actually, of course, the regional employees, having worked on the same material in several states, were in a position to enrich the work in the several states on the basis of their wider experiences.

Original Project Statement

Although, as the Project progressed, numerous modifications were made in the plans as outlined in the first official Project statement, the original Project statement is herewith quoted partly as a matter of record, but more particularly as a bench mark in the development of cooperation in the region. It should be pointed out that this is not submitted as a model Project statement. It did, however, serve as a working base for the latter stages of Project development.

FOR A STUDY OF LAND TENURE IN SOUTHWESTERN STATES WITH EMPHASIS ON THE IMPACTS OF GOVERNMENT PROGRAMS AND OTHER FACTORS

OBJECTIVE: The objective is to determine land tenure changes occurring in recent years as to number of families and labor supply on farms, shifts in tenure status, farming systems and incomes, levels of living, group and community participation, and services of economic and social institutions, in particular reference to the effects of federal and state programs relating to agriculture and rural life.

METHOD: The method will include the use of local survey data representative of major type-situations and more general information obtainable from primary and secondary sources relating to agriculture, the farm population, and the several federal and state programs operating in the region.

The major type-situations, as determined by relative importance in agriculture and having homogeneous tenure characteristics, to be studied relatively intensively are the following:

1. Delta or alluvial flood plains adjacent to the Mississippi River and its tributaries (confined principally to Mississippi, Arkansas, and Louisiana).

2. The Black Prairie (Texas).

3. The Coastal Plain (Mississippi, Louisiana, Arkansas, and Texas).

4. Semi-arid, low plains (Oklahoma and Texas).

5. Rice areas (Arkansas, Louisiana, and Texas).

In addition to the major type-situations, certain minor areas will receive attention according to relative tenure significance, information at hand, or resources available for further study. The more important of these are the following: The Ozark-Ouachita region in Arkansas and Oklahoma, cross timbers in Oklahoma and Texas, foothills in central Arkansas and northern Mississippi, flatwoods in Louisiana and Mississippi, Gulf coastal prairie in Texas, Louisiana, and Mississippi, loessal soil type areas in Arkansas, Louisiana, and Mississippi, etc.

The basic facts for tenure analysis and interpretation are to be obtained by means of the following methods and projects:

A. *Use of available materials and follow-up surveys.*

1. Materials on land tenure available in the region will be assembled and used, and other research materials, such as farm management and general survey data, will be reworked for tenure significance.

2. Follow-up surveys will be made on the same area and farm basis as earlier studies, for determining historical change and as a means of utilizing prior investigations for the regional project.

B. *Intensive local surveys.* One or more local areas consisting of one or more counties in each of the major type-situations designated above, will be selected for intensive study.

1. Detailed information will be obtained from farmers and others, by personal interview and questionnaire method, relating to conditions and changes in respect to

(a) Number and composition of resident families and use made of nonresident labor.

(b) Size of farm, land use, enterprise organization, and physical production by important types of products.

(c) Net returns per farm or per family, cash and non-cash, including wage labor families.

(d) Credit practices and existing indebtedness as related to stability in tenure status.

(e) Net worth.

(f) Landlord-tenant and employer-employee contracts and relations.

(g) Methods of farm production.

(h) Methods of soil improvement and conservation.

(i) Use made of income for food, clothing, shelter, and other specified purposes.

(j) Mobility.

(k) Community and institutional participation and attitudes.

For the foregoing, the sample will be taken in such manner as to obtain adequate coverage for AAA and substantial coverage for Farm Security Administration, Soil Conservation Service, and other agencies, wherever practicable.

2. General information will be collected from the community at large concerning the organization and functioning of

(a) Community institutions (schools, churches, etc.).

(b) Public aid, health services, etc.

(c) Agricultural cooperatives.

(d) Other group activities or services.

The foregoing information is to be collected by means of follow-up surveys in areas previously studied and/or by means of case studies traced back historically.

In some situations it may not be possible to obtain complete data on all phases as listed.

C. *Special sample studies*

1. Clients of the Farm Security Administration. Since the rehabilitation clients of the Farm Security Administration are given direct assistance in farm plans, family budgets, and in other respects, it is proposed to make a special study of this program, on a sample basis and in comparison with other farmers of similar characteristics, by obtaining survey schedules for individual families in practically the same form as those provided for in B. 1. (a to k).

Schedules will be obtained to represent, by tenure and color, three phases of the Farm Security program: community settlements, infiltrated resettlement, and rehabilitation loans. In addition, sample studies will be made of the several types of cooperative associations sponsored by the Farm Security Administration.

2. Cooperators of the Soil Conservation Service. The methods of the Soil Conservation Service involve the replanning of land use and farm enterprises, which, in many parts of the South, may result in shifting lands from cultivated crops to pastures and forestry. It is proposed to study, on a sample basis, the effect of this program on the number of resident families on the land, before and after conservation planning, and the effect on the tenure classes.

D. *General study of all federal and state programs.* It is proposed to make an over-all study of all federal and state programs relating to agriculture and rural life, by means of information to be obtained from the agencies or elsewhere, for the purpose partly of making general application of the local intensive studies and partly for comparing the suitability or adaptability of the respective programs to the several type-situations in the region.

The agencies or functions to be studied in this manner will include the Agricultural Adjustment Administration, the Farm Security Administration, Soil Conservation Service, Work Projects Administration, National Youth Administration, Surplus Commodity Distribution, Farm Credit Administration, Public Health services, rural electrification, the Agricultural Extension Service, county land use and program planning, public education, state and local taxation, federal and state land policies, laws governing tenure relationships, etc.

The intensity of this coverage will depend upon the cooperation of the agencies or the existence of information already available which can be localized for use in the regional project.

COOPERATION: The Departments of Agricultural Economics and Rural Sociology in the five land-grant colleges, in cooperation with the U. S. Bureau of Agricultural Economics, propose to cooperate on the regional project and to coordinate the effort throughout the region. In the study of the major type-situations overlapping state lines, divisions of labor will be used to avoid duplication of effort. The Regional Project will be under the general direction of the Southwestern Land Tenure Research Committee. Regional committees, according to academic training and interest, will be set up to sponsor major subject-matter phases. It is proposed to request the Farm Foundation to assist in coordinating and facilitating the regional cooperation, and it is also proposed to request a grant-in-aid from the General Education Board.

DURATION: Three years.

PUBLICATIONS: It is intended that the agricultural experiment stations will utilize the results obtained in the regional study for their regular series of research publications. It is proposed in addition, however, provided outside funds are made available, to publish one or more regional reports under the sponsorship of the regional research committee.

BUDGET REQUIREMENT: The budget has been estimated on the basis of requirements for (a) field investigations, (b) statistical and clerical, (c) general supervision and preparation of reports,

(d) miscellaneous equipment and supplies, and (e) publishing reports. Attached, in the "Budget Requirements," are shown the proposed contributions of college departments, the Bureau of Agricultural Economics, and the Farm Foundation distributed among the several requirements listed, and an estimate of the minimum amount of additional aid needed to complete the project in three years.

This general plan was followed out although it was curtailed somewhat because of the force of various circumstances, the chief of which were lack of funds and time to complete all that had been planned. From a subject matter standpoint, however, considerable alterations were made in the objective. This naturally had far-reaching consequences and resulted in some confusion. The major alteration concerned putting less emphasis on tenure change and more on the present tenure picture. This shift in emphasis evolved slowly and mainly as a result of the difficulty encountered in the schedule committees of arriving at suitable survey measures which would adequately measure change. Essentially, the general pattern of the Project was that of a cross sectional survey. The attempt to bring in the detail of the changes which had occurred over a period of years posed a particularly difficult problem.

Consequently, without altering the official statement the trend of the actual investigation was altered as the study progressed, particularly in the formation of the schedule. This change was not immediately recorded in the official Project statement and resulted in some uncertainty for a time as to the actual research goals.

The enumeration went much more slowly than had been expected, because of the length and complexity of the schedule. This contingency, however, had been in part anticipated, so that limiting the scope of the study after it was under way did not seriously impair the general plans. As the study progressed, the Committee was confronted with a decision as to whether to curtail the size of the schedule and cover all of the areas originally selected or to gather all the schedule information in a smaller number of areas. The latter course was decided upon. In the main, this meant that the rice areas in the states of Arkansas, Louisiana, and Texas were omitted from the sample.

The result was that the intensive survey (use of the farm and family schedule) was carried on in the following areas: Arkansas

Coastal Plain (Western); Louisiana Coastal Plain (Western);
Mississippi Coastal Plain (Eastern); Oklahoma Rolling Plain;
Texas Blackland Prairie.

Sampling

After having selected the sub-regions in which to carry on the
study, the Regional Committee further narrowed the areas for
purposes of intensive observations. Accordingly, typical counties
were selected within each of the sub-regions. This was done in the
Regional Committee meetings and by the individual committee
members in consultation with the members of their departments.
These counties were selected as samples of sub-regions rather than
of states. Most of the sub-regions transcended state lines.

Although the selection of the counties was done by the Regional
Committee, the selection of the specific families to be interviewed
was done by the individual states under certain general instructions
from the regional office. No two states followed the same procedure. However, these differences entailed no serious scientific
limitation on the materials for regional use, particularly in view
of the fact that the study was concerned with *relationships* rather
than with descriptions of the universes. In some respects, the variations in sampling enriched the regional data, although it made
them somewhat harder to handle.

One of the ever present problems of regional cooperative research is to allow each state the maximum amount of free play
and at the same time to collect comparable information for regional purposes. In the matter of sampling, although identical information was to be collected in each state, it was soon learned that, for
various reasons, no two states wanted to use the same method of
selecting the individual sample families. The reasons given were
presumably valid for the individual states, considering the differences in tenure arrangements, population composition, previous
studies available, and supplementary materials desired for the completion of individual state studies. In order that the procedure at
this point may be better understood, the sampling methods in each
of the states is indicated in some detail.

Arkansas. The Arkansas sample consists of a contiguous area
of Coastal-Plains type soil in Nevada, Columbia, and Union
counties. Excluded from this were bottom land areas along the
Missouri, Ouachita, and Dorcheat Rivers, and the areas of concen-

trated oil development, mainly forest lands. Communities only partially within the sample area were also excluded. By the use of community and neighborhood maps prepared by the Agricultural Extension Service, alternate neighborhoods were selected for the primary sample and the remaining neighborhoods used for substitutions and to supplement certain type situations.

By a stratified, purposeful type of sampling the object was to get one hundred cases in each of five major tenure groups: white owners; white renters; Negro owners; Negro renters; and Negro croppers. In addition, all white croppers, known to be few in the area, were interviewed but the resulting number of cases proved insufficient for extended statistical analysis.

As each neighborhood was selected for sampling, a reconnaissance survey was made with the assistance of local leaders listing the name, color, and tenure of each family in the neighborhood. From the resulting lists it was determined that one-sixth of the white owners and one-third of the other major types should be interviewed in each neighborhood. Accordingly, every third, or sixth, case on the lists was selected for interview. However, because of transportation difficulties some of the more distant neighborhoods were omitted from the sample and alternate neighborhoods closer to headquarters were substituted. Of a total of 87 neighborhoods in the sample area of the three counties, schedules were taken in 46, of which 7 were alternate neighborhoods. In order to describe the tenure universe in the sample area under consideration, it has been determined that the weighting of the cases interviewed should be adjusted as follows: white owners, 2; white renters, 1; white croppers, 3; Negro owners, 1; Negro renters, 1; Negro croppers, 1.

Louisiana. Following conferences with members of parish agricultural planning committeemen and other planning groups of the Extension Service the following community centers conventionally used for extension and other meetings were selected: Lincoln Parish, Hilly; Bienville Parish, Bryceland; Winn Parish, Gaar's Mill; Jackson Parish, Weston.

The selection of cases within these communities was based on complete enumeration of the rural population regardless of tenure status or occupation. Interviewing began at the community center and progressed outward. Approximately one hundred schedules were taken in each area. The cases interviewed are identified with one or the other of the thirteen minor trade centers within the community areas in question.

Mississippi. Jefferson Davis and Marion counties in the Longleaf Pine Area of Mississippi were selected as sample areas. Using neighborhood and community maps prepared by the Agricultural Extension Service, twenty sample neighborhoods were selected by taking every fifth neighborhood in Marion County and every fourth one in Jefferson Davis. The neighborhoods were first numbered from left to right and several trials were made to get areas which were not contiguous and areas which represented different type situations of tenure, soils, type-of-farming, race combinations, and opportunity for off-farm employment. Some of the neighborhoods as delineated were relatively large in area and population. These were divided by noting the clustering of houses on the map, into areas approximating twenty houses each. The selection of these sub-neighborhoods was based on chance.

This procedure resulted in eleven areas in Marion and nine in Jefferson Davis County with a calculated total sample of 400 cases. An attempt was made to interview every family, regardless of tenure status, within the selected areas.

Oklahoma. The Oklahoma sample consisted of a quadrangle-shaped area approximately thirty miles wide by fifty-five miles long and comprised the total of Jackson County, Looney Township in Harmon County, Tilley and Quartz Townships in Greer County, Mountain Park Township in Kiowa County, and Hunter, Maguire, Hazel and Richard Townships in Tillman County. The plan was to sample the entire rural population irrespective of occupation or tenure status. To this end a grid method of sampling was applied utilizing a series of diagonal and cross lines drawn across the map of the quadrangle shaped area at four-mile intervals. Schedules were to be taken on the two families living closest to each line intersection.

It was originally hoped that a sample of farm operators living in villages might be included by this method, but as the plan worked out none of the points fell within the town limits of a village and no substitutions in this regard were made. The general sampling plan, however, was modified within the area of the proposed Altus-Lugart Irrigation Project where three instead of two schedules were taken at each intersection.

Texas. The area chosen was that part of Bell County which represents the Blackland Prairie. The Blacklands of Bell County are not contiguous and for this sample only that part located in the northeastern part of the county was selected. Although erosion varied somewhat, it was attempted to keep the variation in soils within the sample area at a minimum. The sample was further restricted by limiting it to certain size groups based on acres in cropland and selected tenures as indicated by Agricultural Adjustment Administration records. In addition, certain materials were available from a former study in the area.

The selection of individual cases was done entirely from Agricultural Adjustment Administration records and considerable time and effort were spent in securing the sample. All 1941 Agricultural Adjustment Administration records for farms clearly within the Houston clay soil area and not on the outskirts of Temple were pulled from the files. Corrections were made for splits and combinations of work sheets. This resulted in 1,222 work sheets from which data on specific crops and land uses as well as tenure, total acres in cropland, name, address, and location were listed on prepared forms. Farms which lay only partly within the sample area were discarded. Partnerships, nonresident operators, and clear cases of estate operatorship were eliminated as being unusual type cases. Those farms of less than fifteen acres of cropland were eliminated as not being bona fide farming operations. Cash renters and "cropper operators" were eliminated as not being numerically significant. This left four tenure groups—full owners, part owners, share renters, and share-cash renters. All farms were classified by acres in cropland into three groups—15-60, 60-120, and over 120 acres. Part owners with less than 60 acres and share-cash renters with over 120 acres were dropped because the group was not numerically significant. This process resulted in a ten-category sample.

Within each category Tippett's Tables of Random Numbers was applied to determine the order of sampling. After the sample was selected, those farmers interviewed in the previous study referred to above were given preference at the top of each list. This method of sampling was intended to give an adequate sample of the major type situations in the sample area. The sampling was by farms rather than by farmers. For example, if an operator who was on a farm in 1941, as shown by the Agricultural Adjustment

Administration records, had moved and a new farmer was on the place in 1942, the new farmer was interviewed. The actual sample varies somewhat from the plan due to changes in size of farm and tenure of operator between the years 1941 and 1942.

The cropper and laborer sample includes all croppers and laborers who were on the operating units selected by the above procedure.

Comparison between states. Apart from the mechanical differences in sampling procedures among the states, they also differ, as may be noted above, in sampling objectives. Arkansas and Texas tended to concentrate on the usual type tenure cases with the view of building up statistically valid samples for these type situations. Unique cases were, therefore, sometimes excluded from the sample. On the other hand Louisiana, Mississippi, and Oklahoma tended to include all classes of tenures, some of which were unique and variant from the common types. To describe adequately some of these variant cases considerable information additional to that requested by the schedule is necessary. In some instances the interviewers obtained this extra-schedule information, in others they did not.

To this observation it should be added that the numerically less important tenure types of the present may be the emerging significant types of the future. Furthermore, it is from these variant cases that new clues for more satisfactory tenure arrangements are frequently obtained.

Therefore, although the sampling procedure of the states is not uniform, the variations probably enrich rather than limit the value of the data as viewed from the regional standpoint, particularly since the objective of the regional analysis is focused upon the study of relationships rather than upon area description. Thus groups of special types of cases, not now sufficiently numerous for valid statistical analysis, are useful either for case studies or for retention, pending the addition of similar cases to the sample for future statistical analysis.

The Project cooperation at this point serves to exemplify how seemingly divergent interests can be brought together in such a way so as to satisfy the needs of all concerned.

CHAPTER THREE

Collecting The Data

Before going into the detail of the outcome of these plans in actual accomplishment, several comments should be made with respect to certain differences of viewpoint which existed among the committee members themselves and between the committee as a whole and the tenure workers of the region.

Although the committee as a group agreed to the terms upon which the supporting funds were granted, that is, to carry on a cooperative regional project, there was some feeling that it would have been better had each state taken its share of the funds and spent them as it saw fit, apart from any regional organization, except perhaps that each state should have studied the same general problem. An extreme interpretation of this view would have been to regard the regional funds simply as additional departmental money for the individual state institutions.

Although this was not the official viewpoint of the Regional Committee, sentiment of this nature was apparently active in prompting the Committee to rule that regional employees were responsible to the state project leader when in the state in question, rather than to regional direction. This regulation, in and of itself, did not prevent coordination of the work between the states, because, though passed by the Committee, it was never fully subscribed to by them and consequently was adhered to only partially. But arising as it did from a feeling that no outside agency should "tell the state what to do," obviously it somewhat curbed the coordinative power of the Committee. The simple plan of the Committee was that of carrying on a unified program between the states, which of course required a goodly amount of give and take. Naturally state reservations to this fundamental principle of action tended to upset the functioning of the cooperative experiment. Each state was a party to making the general rules of procedure, but once a decision was made, each state was supposed to adhere to it.

It should be borne in mind, of course, that the Project might have been set up to require little collaboration between the states. This, however, was not the case. The Project machinery was geared to a very close collaboration, deviations from which militated against its success.

A second project concern, closely related to the above, was the tendency to use the Project simply as an aid to departmental work, regardless of the interest in the project subject matter, that is, land tenure. This was an extremely subtle force, which probably affected in greater or less degree everyone connected with the project. It acted on the schedule committee meetings and in fact on most of the earlier subject matter deliberations of the Project. This is not to say that the members of the schedule committees, for example, failed to address themselves to the central theme of the Project. There was, however, as the schedule shows, a strong tendency for these committees, particularly in their earlier deliberations, to think in terms of promoting their several subject matter fields rather than in terms of the particular problem of the tenure project. This is partially explainable on the basis of the broadness of the field of tenure, which offered an excellent opportunity for those of varied interests to feel that they could get materials for their own particular uses from a tenure study. Had the subject of the Project been one of narrower scope this difficulty would doubtless have been encountered to a lesser degree. As it was, it was difficult, particularly in the earlier stages of the Project, to bring the focal points of tenure analysis to the fore as clearly as should have been done.

Another of the subtle difficulties encountered in the conduct of the Project concerned the relation of the Regional Committee to the tenure workers of the region. The history of the Regional Project, mentioned earlier in this report, shows that the Project came about as a growth over a period of years incident to the meetings of the group now known as the Regional Committee. At these meetings a great deal of enthusiasm for regional work and for a tenure study in particular had been generated. Especially was this true at the time the present Project was being contemplated. Unfortunately, the enthusiasm generated at these committee meetings was not adequately carried over to the department members—the tenure workers who were to do the actual work of the Project. Although the younger members of the departments were interested and inclined to be agreeable to such a development, they were not sufficiently informed and "sold" on the work and its possibilities. To a number of the younger men, the regional concept meant relatively little. This, coupled with the subject matter of tenure to which only a few had given serious thought, did not stir great enthusiasms in them. The Project was well along before a number of those who were to do the work had really generated the enthusiasm to carry the Project effectively.

Closely related to the above was a lack of definition of the role of the Regional Committee as constrasted with that of the tenure workers. Until rather late in the Project it was not clear that the role of the Committee was chiefly that of a sponsoring and policy group rather than one which anticipated dealing with the detail of the research materials.

For several reasons the formation of the field survey schedule was one of the more difficult phases of regional cooperation. For one thing, it necessarily came early in the development of the Project when the techniques of collaboration had not yet been well-developed. Yet this work was of a most exacting nature and determined the whole future course of the study. In view of the importance of this phase of the Project development it is discussed in some detail. Below is a list of the events as they occurred in developing the regional schedule. Each is discussed more fully in the following pages.

FORMING THE SCHEDULE[1]

1. First schedule committee meeting, Little Rock, November 3 and 4, 1941.

2. Schedules drawn up at Little Rock meeting (landlord, tenant, sociology, and farm management) sent to state departments for comments.

3. Second schedule committee meeting at Texarkana, December, 1941.

1. A printed copy of the Farm and Family Schedule as used in the project may be obtained from The Farm Foundation, 600 South Michigan Avenue, Chicago, Illinois.

4. Meeting of a small group at Baton Rouge, Louisiana, March 26 and 27, 1942, preparatory to the Dallas committee and departmental meeting.

5. Meeting of Regional Committee and all interested state department members at Dallas, April 1 and 2, 1942.

6. Third schedule committee meeting at Fayetteville, Arkansas, April 12 and 13, 1942.

7. Submission of Fayetteville schedule to state departments of Agricultural Economics and Rural Sociology.

8. Fayetteville Regional Committee meeting May 7 and 8, 1942.

9. Schedule taken to the field June 8, 1942.

At the outset, three schedule sub-committees were appointed by the committee chairman, one for Sociology, one for Landlord-Tenant Contracts and Relations and one for Farm Management. These schedule sub-committees were made up of members of the departments of the cooperating state colleges, other than the Regional Committee members, and the Bureau of Agricultural Economics. The general plan contemplated that the Regional Committee would later review and coordinate the work of the schedule sub-committees.

In calling the first schedule committee meeting the Regional Committee chairman indicated that its purpose was "to take steps immediately to prepare and agree upon basic field schedules for the Project." The funds for the Project had not yet been granted, but Arkansas desired to make a study in the upper Ozark region before the first of the year. Oklahoma also wished to start a similar study as soon as possible. Both studies were to be made regardless of a possible grant and according to the committee chairman's statement it "is especially desirable that they conform in every detail to the methods to be used for the regional project. In this way, we expect to experiment with the schedule, sampling process, etc., and thus avoid delays in formulating schedules, etc., after the grant of funds is made, if it is made."

Commenting further on the purpose of the schedule meeting, the Regional Committee chairman stated that "the intention is to first devise schedules for the phases involved in B. 1. (a-k)." (See statement under Project Working Plan for outline of the first official Project plan.) Three schedule sub-committees were then set up as above indicated and a meeting was called at Little Rock, November 3 and 4, 1941.

It was further proposed that these three committees "set up and recommend what they consider complete schedules for their respective phases and also to set up corresponding short schedules for such phases as may need short schedules such as landlord-tenant contracts, farm credit practices, methods of soil improvement and soil conservation or others."

Following the completion of these schedules it was contemplated that the chairmen of the three committees would consider all schedules with a view to determining complete coverage and eliminating duplication. The resulting product was then to be presented to the Regional Committee. In further comment on the schedule committees, the Regional Committee chairman pointed out that he had avoided the appointment of any of the members of the Regional Committee, except in one case, in order to spread the work as much as possible.

A most serious difficulty at this stage of the Project development concerned the definition of the field of tenure as related to the objectives of the Project. A subject difficult of concise limitation and definition under any conditions, the problem became even greater under the particular circumstances of the Project development. The subject of land tenure had been agreed upon, but considerable variation existed among the committee members regarding the phases of the subject that should be emphasized. Moreover, the sentiment was rather strong that it was good policy to keep the definition of the objective broad in order to interest the greatest number of the members of the State Agricultural College departments. While at the time this view appeared to be quite logical, the subsequent difficulty encountered in focalizing the Project research goals indicates the questionability of such procedure. In order to reduce the research goals of the Project to manageable proportions it was eventually necessary anyway to eliminate those phases which did not contribute to the focal points of Project interest.

At any rate, the members of the first schedule committee came together with an exceedingly broad definition of purpose. Although the stated objective of the study was later considerably altered, the schedules developed at this first meeting carried a great deal of weight in the formation of the final schedule.

In noting this organizational set-up, several observations may be made: (1) Although the Regional Committee had met numerous times and discussed the possibilities of a tenure study, the schedule committees did not have the benefit of this background. In other words, they met without really knowing in an effective way what was expected of them. (2) Although the objective of the Project had been stated, it was couched in broad terms, and was consequently an insufficient guide for schedule construction. (3) The subject matter specialists (land economics, farm management, and rural sociology) were segregated in their committee work. They were requested to bring to the meeting the schedules which had been used in their respective fields. Under these instructions the thought tended not to be centered on land tenure but rather on including within the study all of the materials usually included within the scope of their special subject matter interests.

Following this committee meeting, the tentative schedules as formulated were submitted to the chairman of the Regional Committee, who had them processed and sent out for criticism to all departments and staff members concerned. On the basis of these criticisms the schedule committees were to make revisions before finally submitting their recommendations to the Regional Committee. This process was to be complete within about a week.

Although there was commendation of the work done by the schedule committees, letters of comment both from schedule committee and regional committee members indicated a considerable feeling of the need for sharpening up the project objectives. The following comments from three letters are indicative.

"Some one or all of the subject matter groups is going to have to forego much of the detailed information desired in its own field if the total project is to be held within the bounds of reason. If the project is allowed to grow without restraint, we may find ourselves working for the project instead of putting the project to work for us. In other words, if we run down all the side alleys in pursuit of every passing gossamer the success of the whole project might be in danger. I doubt if we fully realize, having acted more or less independently in the formulation of schedules, just how voluminous the combined schedules will be."

"I have several objections to the schedule, the main one being that it does not show signs of being integrated sufficiently about the problems of land tenure. It might serve any purpose for which cooperative schedules on socio-economic conditions in agriculture are used equally as well as the purpose for which it was supposed to have been designed."

"I feel that if we are going to study land tenure we have got to study land tenure and forget about all the by-products that may be got out of the study. For example, the farm-management people want labor income and rate earned; the land economists want number of acres devoted to every kind of crop or weed that grows; and the sociologists are supposed to want to know if everybody has a screened porch . . . "

The writer of the final letter above points out that in this way the schedule lacks unity, having a little section of this and another on that, according to the particular interests of the subject matter fields, and concludes by saying: "If, in view of all these considerations, you have some time to spend on this schedule I hope you can find it possible to spend some of that time trying to integrate that schedule about some one center, main, predominant problem. That should be land tenure."

Second Schedule Committee Meeting

In view of the various suggestions for schedule changes, some of them of a rather fundamental nature, a second schedule committee meeting was held in Texarkana in December, 1941. This was rather an informal meeting, with some turnover in personnel from the first meeting. Also several of the regional committee members were present. Not much change was made in the detail of the schedules, the main discussion centering around the major objectives of the study. Up to this time, the major objective of the study centered around tenure change and the effect of government programs. The schedules resulting from the first schedule committee, however, contained little that would yield definite information of this nature, hence the question of whether or not the objective should be modified was increasingly discussed.

For several reasons, as has already been intimated, the first schedule committee did not adhere strictly to the statement of the objectives: (1) The objectives were stated very broadly and it was not clear what was to be stressed. (2) Schedule committee members had not been "sold" on a tenure study. They were more interested in making studies in their own subject matter fields than in the field of tenure, hence there was a tendency to use the tenure study as a means to an end. (3) The committee members brought various copies of their old standard subject matter schedules with them. As a result there was a tendency to try to effect the inclusion of whole sections of these schedules without sufficient regard for their orientation to the field of tenure. (4) In addition to not being "sold" on the tenure study in general, the schedule committee members were also not convinced that the tenure change and government aspects of the study were of primary importance. (5) Finally, this particular type of information appeared to be difficult to obtain and, in fact, probably out of reach in the type of survey contemplated.

Although there were those at the second schedule committee meeting who argued for the retention of tenure change and government programs as major features of the study, these phases were never stressed after this meeting, although no substitute objectives were immediately adopted.

Steering Committee Meeting

Following the second schedule committee meeting it was determined that it would be desirable to have a meeting of the combined departments of rural economics and sociology together with the Regional Committee in a general meeting to discuss the plans for the Regional Project. Accordingly, this meeting convened in Dallas, April 1 and 2, 1942.

Prior to this general meeting a steering committee met in Baton Rouge, March 26 and 27, for the purpose of drawing up plans for the general meeting. In view of the fact that the working objectives of the Project seemed not to have been clear to the schedule committees, it was deemed advisable to reword the Project statement and develop somewhat of a different approach than had been presented in the previous official statement. The following is the statement which this committee issued:

A STUDY OF LAND TENURE IN THE SOUTHWESTERN STATES

DEFINITION: For the purpose of this study land tenure is defined as the manner in which rights to use and occupy land and to enjoy income from land are shared between various individuals and society. The relationship among all individuals who share any rights to land is thus considered in the concept of land tenure as used here.

HYPOTHESIS AND STATEMENT OF PROBLEMS: Land tenure is a fundamental issue in the solution of the following problems of agriculture:

1. Low levels of income for farm families.

2. Mal-distribution of farm income.

3. Lack of opportunity for farm families to improve their economic status.

4. Low levels of social development.

5. Lack of opportunity for farm families to improve their social status.

6. Land resource wastage and devastation.

7. Inefficient and inadequate production.

8. Low level of health and nutrition.

OBJECTIVE: To establish and determine:
1. Causal relationship of tenure factors to above problems.

2. Extent to which tenure factors are barriers or impediments to proper solution of these problems.

3. Adjustments in tenure which are required in order to solve these problems.

METHOD: The general research and study approach should be as follows:

1. Determine causal relationship of tenure to each of these problems by comparing the performance as to level of labor income, level of social development, efficiency of production, distribution of income, rate of soil depletion and erosion, etc., under varying tenure systems as found in separate areas where distinct variations exist in tenure factors as distribution of control, legal, economic, and social relationship between those who have control, and manner in which controls are exercised while holding constant factors other than tenure that have a causal relationship to performance—thus leaving a residue which may be assumed to be due to the difference noted in the tenure factors.

2. Check performance as above on sample farms and areas at two separate intervals of time during which tenure conditions have changed, using for this purpose either some historical period and the current period or the current period and some future period, whichever is feasible.

3. Determine the degree of achievement under varying tenure systems of uniformly administered programs designed to mitigate one or more of the agricultural problems with which this Project is concerned as a means of establishing the extent and manner in which tenure acts as a barrier to the programs.

4. Determine the changes that have occurred in tenure resulting from agricultural programs in areas where a uniform system of tenure exists by comparing tenure changes on farms affected by or participating in such programs with farms not affected by or participating in such programs.

5. Appraise the accomplishment of existing tenure reform and adjustment programs in light of what is shown to be needed from the above determinations.

6. On the basis of the above determinations and appraisals develop the adjustments in tenure that will likely eliminate it as a cause of agricultural problems.

7. On the basis of the above determinations and appraisals derive the tenure adjustments most likely to minimize it as a barrier to the solution of these problems.

MINIMUM FACTS NEEDED: To resolve adequately the hypothesis of the Project and to make such other determinations as are necessary, the following categories of information will be required:

1. Levels of labor income for each segment of the agricultural labor force, for each farm and area under study.

2. Levels of social attainment for each farm and area under study, for each segment of the whole agricultural labor force.

3. Historical record of occupational mobility of each segment of the whole agricultural labor force.

4. Parties interested in land and extent of control over use, occupancy, and income exercised by each according to size and tenure of farms.

5. Current record of the distribution of real income from agriculture among all interested parties for each farm and area under consideration.

6. Record of persistent land-devastation farming practices associated with each farm and area under consideration.

7. Record of how each agricultural program operates on each farm and in each area under study.

8. Record of how each tenure improvement program operates on each farm and in each area under study.

METHODS OF OBTAINING FACTS: The facts required for this study should be obtained according to the following principles:

1. Facts to be obtained from primary sources should be gathered in precise and accurate manner.

2. No facts that are reasonably reliable and available in secondary sources should be gathered from primary sources. For example, in records of crop acreage, any yields if considered warranted should be taken from AAA records rather than through interviews with farmers.

3. Estimates of facts should never be relied upon when actual facts can be ascertained.

4. Minuteness of detail on facts is not necessary to guarantee accurateness.

With these principles as guides facts should be gathered as follows:

1. Control of land facts from courthouse and AAA records including such information as operating pattern to reveal tenant control, ownership pattern to reveal owner control, record of mortgage debt to reveal credit controls, etc.

2. Farm practice and income data from AAA and FSA case records.

3. Social attainment levels from school records, survey of community patterns, etc.

4. Detailed operational records of agricultural programs from local administrative personnel.

5. Information on occupational mobility, personal relationships like landlord-tenant relationships, managerial practices, farmer opinions and attitudes, land owner opinions and attitudes, and similar information unavailable elsewhere from personal interviews.

AREAS IN WHICH TO OBTAIN FACTS: No definite predetermined group of areas should be selected. Each separate area studied should provide significant distinct variations from any other area so far as tenure factors are concerned. Significant variation so far as type of farming is concerned is, for example, not sufficient unless there are also significant variations in tenure factors. In each area after the first one is selected, succeeding areas should be selected only after preliminary surveys to establish the character of its variations from areas previously selected.

Meeting of Regional Committee and All
State Department Members

In opening this meeting the chairman of the Regional Committee indicated that the Committee had accepted funds from the General Education Board and the Farm Foundation with the understanding that it would deliver a completed project. He indicated that there would be many different points of view in the states and many different philosophies to bring together and that it was important that the Project develop an interest in the region as well as in the individual states. He went on to say that the development of the regional phase would be difficult since there were no precedents to follow and that in such a cooperative undertaking the democratic process should prevail at all times. He further warned that it would undoubtedly be impossible to secure all of the information that each member of the committee would like to have for a complete study within his own line of interest but that a successful project would serve as a basis for future studies. The meeting was then turned over to the incoming Project Director with the request that he outline all the objectives and facts required in the Project.

At the time of this meeting the Project Director was just taking over his duties. What had gone before had transpired without the benefit of a central working organization. In retrospect, it appears that it would have been highly desirable for the director to have been on the job much earlier than was the case. In an undertaking so large, much detailed clearance is necessary and naturally full time effort is needed. In addition, a functionary was needed to fill the gap between the Regional Committee and the members of the several departments. The Committee up to this time had been the coordinating agency, but the tenure workers in the several departments to whom the work of the Project was to fall had not effectively felt the responsibility of shouldering the work of the Project. Cooperation on the level of Regional Committee planning had long been under way but a regional cooperation among the research workers who were to carry the burden of the research had not come into being. Such cooperation did not actually come into being until, as later described, the First Workers' Conference.

The history of the Project to this point indicates that the thinking of the department members in the various states had been largely in terms of their own local projects and subject matter fields and had not been oriented to the regional land tenure study to any considerable extent. Moreover, the representatives of the several subject matter fields had been rather sharply critical of each other, each feeling that most of the answers resided within the scope of his subject matter and that the others were not essential to a study of this type. This particular meeting was crucial in the development of the Project in that it brought together all of the department and committee members for the first time for the purpose of considering project procedure. Apart from purely subject matter considerations it was felt that possibly the chief objective for this meeting concerned the coordination of the efforts of those representing the three subject matter fields and at the same time emphasizing that each person present was a part of a regional cooperative endeavor.

The first question raised was: What are the fundamental problems in southern agriculture? As problems were mentioned, they were followed with the question: Is this problem directly related to tenure? If so, it was then placed upon the board as a focal point of study for the Project. After eight major problems were listed (they were essentially the same as those listed in the above outline prepared by the steering committee), the question was then raised as to the ability of the disciplines represented in the departments to furnish information on the questions and problems raised.

This procedure tended to get a work objective out in front of the group so that the members left off being critical of each other's particular approaches and fields and commenced to assess their own subject matter resources and techniques to see what each could contribute to the solution of the indicated problems. The term "problem" as used referred primarily not to methods of alleviation but was utilized rather to serve as a guide to direct the scope and content of the research to be undertaken. For example, low income was the first problem listed. All agreed that here was a phase of southern agriculture which was related to tenure and one on which study should be directed.

Discussion of the problems soon revealed that they had many angles, showed great variation in the several parts of the region, and could not be adequately treated from the viewpoint of any single discipline represented. This general approach of centering on problems to be solved, introduced a certain amount of humility into the representatives of the several subject matter specialties particularly when they were confronted specifically with the question of what their discipline could contribute toward the understanding of the relation of tenure to the problem at hand. In a subsequent session of the department members, at which the committee members were not present, a good spirit of cooperation between the subject matter fields was developed. This was a decided step in advance in the research cooperation of the group. As a result the department members generated a considerable amount of enthusiasm for the Project. It should be pointed out that this grew out of the subject matter discussion as oriented to land tenure. The representatives of the several disciplines rather suddenly realized that their efforts were related and complementary and that the several subject matter fields were necessary for a proper comprehension of the problem at hand. Moreover, the advantages of regional collaboration became much more evident than they had been before.

Third Schedule Committee Meeting

In order to consolidate the suggestions from the Dallas meeting, a schedule committee meeting was called for Fayetteville for April 12 and 13. The task of achieving a working unanimity of opinion with so large a group of people representing several subject matter fields and areas should not be underestimated. Although the meeting proved to be a fruitful one, several organizational limitations should be noted. In at least three and possibly four of the states, the schedule committee representatives were either not authorized or were not otherwise in position to represent the thinking in their states. One of the state representatives was only on temporary employment and did not intend to take part in the actual work of the study. Hence he felt that he could not speak for the state, and in fact, was only in part-time attendance at the meetings. At the other extreme, one of the state representatives spoke for his state rather freely, but a number of his opinions were reversed later by the department which he was attempting to represent.

This meeting was the first real attempt at a coordination on the survey schedule of the subject matter fields with the subject of land tenure as the definite orientation. There was no official chairman and the group proceeded informally as a group, not as three subject matter fields. An outline of the points that should be considered in the schedule as a whole was worked out on a blackboard. This procedure proved to be effective and helpful.

Following this meeting several regional employees, who had recently come on the job, made the revisions in the schedules as suggested by the meeting and sent them out to the states for criticism, pending the final acceptance of the schedule by the Regional Committee which was to meet in Fayetteville, May 7 and 8, in about three weeks' time.

The Fayetteville Committee Meeting, May 7 and 8

Prior to this meeting, members of the staffs at each of the institutions had gone over the schedule (*Regional Tenure Study*, 4/18/42) submitted by the third schedule committee and had made suggestions for corrections. Some of these suggestions were made directly to the members of the regional staff and others were brought along by the Regional Committee members to the meeting. In the main, however, these suggestions were of a rather minor nature. The schedule committee, however, had tried to reconcile the divergent views held by members of the Regional Committee and others with respect to the collection of farm management data. A comparison of the schedule as revised by the committee (*Regional Tenure Study, Revised, 5/14/42*) with the schedule mentioned above shows the extent of these revisions. The changes were mainly additions, made in an effort to provide flexibility of procedure by the states as a means of reaching an agreement. The schedule as adopted at this meeting was henceforth the official project schedule.

Since this matter has a bearing on the subsequent conduct of the Project, and on the conduct of projects in general, it may be well at this point to use it as an example to indicate more specifically the type of difficulty which situations of this kind create. The original difficulty arose from a difference of opinion among the farm management representatives as to the proper method of handling income and expense data. All were agreed, including committee members, that a net farm income figure was desirable, but the differences in method by which this figure was to be obtained were not resolved. As a result, the regional schedule as adopted did not include the necessary questions to arrive at a net income figure, by either of the several methods suggested. In view of this the states added to their state schedules and followed their own methods in this regard, Texas using a budgetary approach and Arkansas a detailed farm account method. The other states ranged somewhere between these two extremes.

State Additions to the Regional Schedule

The regional schedule as herein referred to is the schedule which was to be used in all of the states. It was understood that it would not be necessary for the states to use identical schedules but each state was to collect all the information contained in the schedule that was passed on by the committees, that is, the regional schedule. Realizing that each state would want to add to this schedule, the Regional Committee at the Fayetteville meeting passed the following resolution: "That each state be permitted to use supplementary sheets with the schedule provided the additional cost is reasonable and securing the additional information does not interfere with the progress of the study."

This additional material was of two general types: (1) Additional blocks of material appended to the schedule, such as war production schedules, practice schedules, etc., which consisted of one or more sheets of information. Getting such information, although possibly desirable in many respects, tended to slow up the work and caused a deterioration in the quality of the regional schedule material. (2) Additional bits of data throughout the body of the regional schedule. In reworking the regional schedule to fit state needs no two states followed the same practices. In Arkansas the regional schedule was used in the field exactly as issued from the Regional Office, except that additional materials were appended to it. Enumerators were instructed, however, to get additional information on various items throughout the schedule but these items were not included in the set-up of the schedule itself. Mississippi left the detail of the regional schedule the same but rearranged it into two sections to fit with the field work interview plan: (1) Tenant, part-owner, and laborer schedule; (2) Owner schedule. To each of these sections was appended the main bulk of the sociological part of the schedule which was taken in separate interview during a considerable part of the survey. Louisiana changed some of the regional schedule detail and rearranged the schedule into three sections: (1) Leasing arrangements; (2) Family composition; (3) Ownership. Oklahoma rearranged the regional schedule throughout by adding to a number of the sections. The schedule was not broken up into smaller units for field work purposes although only a part of the information of the schedule was taken at any one interview. Texas rearranged the sections of the regional schedule but carried the same lettering as the original regional schedule. Except for two sections the detail was not changed greatly. Regardless of state changes in detail of the regional schedule all states in one way or another got certain additional materials. These additions varied according to the needs of the state in question.

In the states where the schedules were entirely remade it was exceedingly difficult for the schedule takers to follow the regional schedule instructions. Consequently, state instructions in conformity with the state schedule had to be worked out. Under these conditions the context of the questions was frequently changed, which tended to give rise to difference in interpretations. In the states using the form as set up by the Regional Office, but adding to it, the addition of items here and there throughout the schedule became quite confusing to the schedule taker, particularly in those cases where blanks for the additional items were not mimeographed in on the schedule form. Yet for certain types of questions, it was scarcely feasible to take them out of their context and append them on a separate sheet at the end of the schedule. The schedule, already complicated, became even more so as the result of these factors.

One of the schedule takers who worked in three of the five states was greatly impressed with the differences in state procedure and took the trouble to make a detailed statement for each state of the items which the schedule taker was supposed to fill in, which were not on the regional form. These were matters of practical importance to the schedule taker. Had he been able to see the difficulty that these items made in the later handling of the data, he would have been even more impressed. This schedule taker's observations included only the materials covered in the first visit in the state in question. This constituted probably slightly more than one-half of the schedule. He went to the trouble to list the detail of each point, which is available in the Project files, but there is submitted here only a summary of his statement. These refer to items in one state not on the mimeographed schedule which he took to the field.

Additions to be made 14
Corrections to be made 4
Times additional space needed 8
Omissions and errors in typing 1
Footnotes expected of enumerator 7
Supplementary sheets 1
Items difficult to secure or impractical of application 2
                                                    —
    Total Items 37

This confusion of items put a strain on the schedule taker which resulted in a distinct diminution in the quality of his work throughout the schedule. Moreover, it made the task of transcribing these schedule data to the regional printed forms a very difficult one. In fact, the transcription of data to the regional printed form was so unsatisfactory that in two of the states it was necessary for the original schedules to be sent to the regional office so that they could be reworked before they could be tabulated. In the case of another state, the task of transcription apparently looked so formidable that the state schedules were sent to the Regional Office without an attempt being made to transcribe them to the regional printed form.

The Schedule Instructions

In any survey using a detailed schedule two items among others are very important: (1) That the schedule be tried out in the field and the necessary corrections made before the actual schedule taking gets under way. (2) That detailed schedule instructions be available to the schedule takers.

These procedures were even more crucial in the Regional Project with its elaborate schedule and five-state scope. The timing of the Project was such, however, that neither of these steps could be carried through with the thoroughness that was desired. At the Fayetteville committee meeting, at which time the final schedule was adopted, four suggestions in this connection were made: (1) That the regional staff revise the survey schedule according to the committee suggestions and send copies to each of the states. (2) That since a majority of those present felt the schedule should be taken at several visits, each state should review the schedule at once and submit to the regional office a statement by survey areas of plans and procedures, dates or months preferred for field work, and suggested groupings for the different segments of the schedule in terms of methods of field work to be used. Upon receiving this information the regional staff should prepare the schedule to be secured in the different visits. All of the states were to obtain their information in the same order suggested by the regional staff. (3) That the regional staff and possibly some of the departments try the survey schedule in the field to determine whether further revisions seemed desirable. (4) That the regional staff prepare detailed instructions for use of the schedule by enumerators.

As already stated, the timing of the field work prohibited carrying these suggestions through. After the Fayetteville committee meeting the schedule was reworked in accordance with the committee instructions. This took a matter of several weeks so that the schedules actually did not reach the states in mimeographed form until around May 20, following the April committee meeting. One of the states, anxious to get the field work under way, immediately set to work upon the regional schedule in adapting it to its purposes and started field work with a number of enumerators on the following June 8. Schedule instructions had not been issued at this time and the rapidity with which the field work progressed in this state precluded the possibility of catching up with the situation. In fact, the bulk of the field work in this state was finished by August 1 and totally discontinued September. 1. Actually the final schedule instructions were not sent out until September 16.

THE FIELD WORK PLAN

Timing the Field Work

In its broad conception the field work plan was relatively simple but because of the wide scope of the Project its application at certain points became somewhat involved.

The general plan included the following major features:

1. That the materials included in the regional schedule be collected uniformly in all states.

2. That the states have the responsibility of collecting these data under the coordination of the Regional Office.

3. That the schedule enumerators be shifted from state to state as the need arose.

4. That when the schedule data were collected, they were to be transcribed in the states to uniform printed regional forms supplied by the Regional Office.

5. That following this transcription the forms be sent to the regional office edited and ready for tabulation. Since the editing and schedule instructions for all states were uniform it was assumed that further adjustment of individual state data or of the data between states to make them comparable would be at a minimum.

In adjusting the field work between the states it became evident at the beginning that the several states were not in an equal stage of readiness to go ahead with the work and also that there was a considerable difference in the speed with which they wished to proceed. Two states began field work in June of 1942, a third was added in July, a fourth in August, and a fifth in September. As already stated, however, the speed in the states varied greatly. In one state, the field work lasted less than three months and in another it ran over a period of more than a year. The other states ranged between. This was partially due to the different sizes of the field crews. In the state which finished in less than three months as many as eleven persons were used at one time, whereas in the one taking the longest time only three persons were employed most of the time. In the case of the latter state, the field work plan contemplated that the field workers would become residents of the area in which they were working. This being the case, the plan of switching the enumerators from one state to the other as the occasion demanded did not apply except at the very end of the work in that state, when it became necessary to complete the work in a rather short time.

The plan of considering the five states as a unit for field work, however, effected certain economies in personnel. The regional office coordinated the shifting of personnel by means of ascertaining in advance the plans of each state with respect to number of personnel needed. Transfers were made accordingly. Some of the enumerators did not go outside of the state in which they began work, while others worked in as many as four states.

There was a considerable advantage in this procedure in that the experiences of the enumerators were enriched by their contacts in several states. The benefits of this were transmitted to the Project in the enumerators' impressions reports which each enumerator was requested to write. These reports comprise 747 pages of typewritten materials for the region as a whole. Another benefit from this procedure was the economy in the training of enumerators. This was of particular importance in view of the complexity of the schedule and the scope of the Project. Even so, a total of 50 enumerators worked on the collection of the data during the course of the Project. For the most part the enumerators employed were experienced persons not only knowing the subject matter but experienced in meeting the public. The master's degree was held as a prerequisite in most instances. There was also a tendency for a given state to improve its methods by being informed in detail as to procedures in the other states.

Under the practical operation of the Project, however, there were some limitations as to the desirability of transferring workers from state to state. The chief of these appears to have been the adjustment of the enumerator to the difference in the methods used, and the material collected in the different states. This, it would seem, is a difficulty inherent not so much in the transfer of workers from state to state, as in the lack of achieving the goal of uniformity between the states set up by the Committee. The discrepancy in work methods between the states probably should not have been so great, but where the methods were diverse, the enumerator passing from one state to another was sure to show it up. As a result, greater uniformity was achieved. However, uniformity achieved in this way came rather hard.

In several of the states, the Project leaders were sensitive about having their attention called to how things were being done in their neighboring state, even though the procedure called to their attention appeared to be superior. The problem possibly lies somewhat deeper and touches again the point of lack of uniformity on certain rather essential matters as between the states. Early in the Project the Regional Committee passed the resolution that whenever a regional or any other employee of the Project came into a given state in the process of collecting survey information he thereby came under the supervision of the Project leader of that state. Correctly interpreted, this ruling would not have hampered cooperative effort between the five states, but carried to an extreme, it made it impossible in several instances for the regional staff to carry out even the decisions of the Regional Committee with respect to achieving uniformities when a given state was obviously out of line. The essential point to be made in this connection is that successful cooperation demands an emotional as well as an intellectual commitment to the principles of cooperation.

An obvious mechanical difficulty involved the various state additions to the regional schedule. This has already been referred to. This difficulty appeared not to be particularly serious except where a considerable amount of material was expected of the enumerator which was not specifically indicated on the schedule as such but was supposed to be interpolated here and there throughout the course of the interview.

Finally, there was the matter of the difference in work methods as between the states. The work instructions of the field leaders varied greatly. In one of the states, the enumerators were given a certain quota of schedules to get and they were expected to get them regardless of the circumstances. The emphasis here was on number of schedules.

In other instances the instructions were to stay with the cases regardless of time, so long as a reasonable number of schedules was taken. The matter of explanatory notes was also a matter of considerable difference between the states. In some instances these were reduced to a bare minimum; in others they were required to be quite elaborate.

The transcribed schedules from the last state to finish its work were sent to the Regional Office in February, 1944. The field work and transcription of data in the states thus covered a period of twenty months.

Methods of Data Collection As Between States

As already intimated, no two of the states went about collecting their data in exactly the same way. These differences were partly due to practical considerations within the states and partly to differences in the theory of research. Several different types stand out.

The first has been dubbed the *commando* method. In this instance the practical consideration was that a number of advanced graduate students were available for only two or three months during the summer and it appeared that these were the only persons available to do the enumeration. Therefore a crew averaging about nine persons was put into the field and the bulk of the survey work was concluded in a little over two months' time. Unfortunately, neither the schedules nor their instructions were completed at the time this intensive field work got under way. Hence the results under the circumstances were not entirely satisfactory. Under other conditions this method might have worked very well. It has the advantage of getting the job over with. Obviously, however, the work procedure needs to be entirely crystallized before the operation begins because little can be done by way of experimentation with such a large force in the field.

A second method was a variety of *participant observer* technique. The plan here was for the enumerators to live in the area in which they were working, thus becoming acquainted with the families selected for interview. Particularly in view of the long schedule where several visits would be necessary anyway, it was thought that this would make possible a number of visits, increase the accuracy of the information as well as afford the possibility of noting changes during the extended period of observation.

It was pointed out that this method would yield more information than where a large group of enumerators were placed in the field for a short period of time. Under this plan the enumerators could get acquainted with the farmers and gain their confidence. The type of enumerator needed in this instance would necessarily be a more highly trained person than one used on a short time basis. In addition to securing the standard schedule information it would be possible for the enumerator while living in the community to obtain considerable background information which would be particularly valuable.

This method was put into operation in the state in question and three enumerators with their families moved into the area. After having lived there for about six months, however, one of the men resigned and another was called to military service. This left only one man to complete the work. It was more than he could do in the allotted length of time. Therefore in April, 1943 two members of the regional staff were sent into the area to help complete the schedule taking. Since the resignations made it impossible to complete the experiment as planned no objective data are at hand to indicate how successful it might have been had conditions been such that the original schedule takers could have completed the task. However, a considerable amount of local information was collected in this area that would not have been obtained otherwise.

A third method of data collection might be called the *cooperator* method. This sought to make cooperators out of the families interviewed, the thought being that as the data were collected, summaries of its content, as available, should be given back to the communities in question. It was thought that this technique would tend to insure better cooperation from the families interviewed and at the same time give a check on the information obtained. In addition it would give a chance to get interpretations of data as they were being presented to the communities. Although this plan is probably better adapted to a long term program of research and extension than to a temporary project, some evidences of its value have been noted. Unfortunately, however, the personnel on the staff in this state also changed during the period and thus the program was interrupted.

The methods used in the states other than those described were of a conventional nature, that is to say, they used field staffs of moderate size and carried on the field work over a period of six or eight months.

The Community Aspects

The foregoing comments respecting the field work have been limited to the data on the farm and family schedules. Reference to the project working plan included earlier in this report indicates two phases of the intensive local survey: (1) data on individual farm families (the Farm and Family Schedule) and (2) information on the functioning of community institutions and other community groups.

Specific schedules were never developed by the schedule committees for obtaining the community information, that is, the second phase. After the project was under way, however, outlines for obtaining such information were developed by the regional staff and presented to the regional committee at its Memphis meeting in January of 1943. These plans were discussed at length at the Second Workers' Conference the following November.

The fact that the Farm and Family Schedule work got under way first and the time ran short probably accounts in the main for the fact that very little was done by any of the state workers on this phase of the subject. Considerable interest was evidenced, however, and nearly all of the sampling was done on a community and neighborhood basis. Several members of the regional staff collected a considerable amount of community and institutional information with the assistance and collaboration of the state workers.

CHAPTER FOUR

Processing The Data

Throughout the planning of the project it was anticipated that most of the tabulation of the data was to be done in the central Regional Office. At the July, 1942 Regional Committee Meeting the matter was discussed in some detail. All of the committee members excepting one or possibly two believed that if uniformity was to be achieved in the analysis the tabulation should be done in this way. It was pointed out, however, that in following this procedure it might be possible and even necessary to "farm out" some of the work to the various states. It was further pointed out that the tabulation of the material in the Regional Office would not interfere with the interpretation of the data by the state project leader. In fact it was thought that regional tabulation would facilitate his work by relieving him of much mechanical detail.

Under this plan the states would not only have access to the tabulations but it was contemplated that the records would be returned to the state after the Regional Office tabulation was completed. The state leader would thus have the privilege of making further analysis if he so desired. It was contemplated at the time of this meeting that the state workers would make up skeleton tables showing the type of tabulation desired so that the Regional Office could fulfill their requests.

Although the general plan as indicated above was carried out, several aspects of the detail were altered. Instead of sending the original state schedules to the Regional Office these schedules were transcribed to the printed regional form in the states. Normally the original schedules of the states were not sent to the Regional Office.

Also, most of the directions for tabulations were submitted to the Regional Office through the workers' conferences rather than from individual workers as such. In this way the tabulation directions were based on the combined judgment of the workers. Descriptions of the workers' conferences appear later in this report.

PROBLEM OF EDITING IN REGIONAL OFFICE

Considerable effort was expended in an attempt to get uniformity of data on all schedules by editing in the Regional Office as well as by field editing and editing done at the time of transcription. This was necessary in the field partially because a total of fifty different enumerators worked at taking schedules in the five states. These enumerators had varying experience from none to over twenty years. Some were born in the area where they enumerated, others had had no experience with the type of farming or kinds of people with whom they were working. Some were exposed to a four day "school for enumerators," while others went to the field with a minimum of instruction. While most of the enumerators were men, a total of six women were employed to enumerate household items. Two Negroes were employed in Mississippi to enumerate Negro cooperators. In some cases as many as three enumerators worked on the same schedule. The different states used slightly different definitions in an attempt to fit the schedule to local conditions and in many instances the same definition was given varying interpretations. However, in so far as possible the Regional Office translated the data to conform to common definitions. Enumeration began in June, 1942 and the last schedule was taken in the summer of 1943.

All editing in the Regional Office was done by staff members or under the close supervision of a staff member. The schedules were edited to fit conceptual definitions which were stated in detail for each item. If the schedule item conformed to the definition, it was passed on. If some other definition was followed, the data were edited to conform to a uniform definition. Many schedules had to be edited to fit the 1942 calendar year as to age, education of those still in school, deaths, births, marriages, and members away from home.

Simple editing was done directly on the schedule and some coding of combinations of items was done directly on the schedule. Other more complicated indexes and summary measures were computed on work sheets and the computed figures copied directly from the work sheets to the master sheets for punching.

The work involved in editing the state schedules so as to make them comparable was much greater than had been anticipated. As already stated, the first step to insure uniformity between the states was the acceptance of a uniform regional schedule. Additional items could be added but nothing was to be taken away.

However, it was obvious that certain items were meaningless in some of the areas. Hence they were omitted. For example, rice was listed on the crop table but since no rice was grown in the area sampled it was omitted from all state field schedules. Since the plantation labor system does not exist in Oklahoma the number of families in the operating unit was omitted. In addition to changes such as these considerable variation occurred in the methods of securing the data, tables were reorganized, and wording was changed. In many cases the changes constituted improvement of the regional schedule but each change pointed the question toward a slightly different objective which rendered comparability difficult.

One variety of such changes consisted in the translation of regional wording to local terminology. Probably more serious, though less apparent, were the differences in definition of specific items. For example, a major series of questions in the schedule deals with leasing arrangements. Were the arrangements to be those agreed upon, those which were actually performed, or both? In this instance each state officially adopted slightly different definitions. In some instances a definition was adopted at the beginning of the enumeration in a given state but was later changed as the enumeration progressed.

The degree of uniformity both within and between the states depended somewhat on the number of contacts between the project leaders in the various states. In the cases where the project leaders were present at the schedule committee conferences a greater tendency toward uniformity existed. In formulating the schedule, reasons were stated as to the purpose of each question, the characteristic it was supposed to measure, and the theory back of the question. The third meeting of the schedule committee in Fayetteville was attended by one representative from each state. At this meeting certain hypotheses were set up which consolidated and gave direction to the work of the previous schedule committees. The members of this meeting were present at the so-called schools for enumerators in the states and were available for counsel at all times, but in only one state was the state representative in the field from the beginning of the enumeration period to the end. This meant that the Project leader in charge of the field crew in four states did not have the benefit of the thinking of the final schedule committee meeting which gave more specific directions than any of the previous meetings had done. Some of the thinking was undoubtedly transmitted from time to time at conferences of staffs and field workers in these states, but discussion of all detail in this way was virtually impossible.

The turnover of enumerators was of course an important factor in securing uniformity or the lack of it. The following compilation shows the number who worked during the entire enumeration.

	Ark.	La.	Miss.	Okla.	Texas
Total Enumerators Employed	16	12	15	12	8
Enumerators Continuing During Entire Enumeration	6	4	4	1	6

Complicating the turnover indicated above was the necessity of making several visits to secure all of the schedule information. This meant that the person taking the first part of the schedule may or may not have completed the schedule which he started, thus introducing an enumerator bias within the schedule. An example of this is exemplified in the interpretation of "kinship to owner." In some instances kinship was relative to the male head and in others to the female head, the latter interpretation being used principally by female enumerators who got the household aspects of the schedule information. This type of error was not too serious but in several cases even the farm tenure status varied between enumerators when the same case was interviewed by two different schedule takers.

The background and educational experience of the enumerators varied greatly. A total of five people local to the area being studied were employed in three of the states. These people had little experience with technical survey problems involved. Out of a total of fifty different enumerators twenty-six were natives of the states in which they worked. Two of these, however, were not natives of the cotton areas of their states and had to be oriented to that type of farming. In one state two local colored people were employed to take schedules on the second visit in two neighborhoods which were entirely colored. Both of these enumerators had M.A. degrees but not in agriculture. While these colored enumerators did excellent work they refused to set down in writing their impressions with respect to the problems encountered.

In addition to those enumerators who were natives of the state in which they worked ten other enumerators were natives of the Cotton South. One of the enumerators was a native of South America and had considerable language difficulty. Eighteen of the enumerators had had no experience with agricultural schedule taking. However, familiarity with former schedules and local situations did not always work for the best. Some of the "old hands" had preconceived notions which were hard to displace. Also some of the local enumerators tended to tell the farmers what the situation was instead by asking them. Only eighteen of the enumerators had previous experience with the State Experiment Stations. Of the total of fifty enumerators nine worked in more than one state, necessitating adjustment to the changes of interpretations as between the states.

Reference has already been made to "enumerator schools." Such schools or conferences were held in all the states. These ran from two to three days at the first of the enumeration period and short sessions of an hour or so were held intermittently on particular problems. Unfortunately, in only one of the states were all enumerators present at these first conferences. In Louisiana one-half of of the enumerators attended the first conference; in Mississippi, one-third; in Oklahoma, one-third; in Arkansas, one-half; in Texas, all.

As other enumerators came into the field it was necessary to break them in one at a time. This was usually done by the field editors. Since this slowed up the work this schooling was often reduced to a minimum. In Oklahoma however a new conference was held when any new enumerator joined the staff, all other work being discontinued until the new enumerator was fully instructed. For the most part the field leaders seemed to believe that the best way for a new enumerator to understand the schedule was to take it to the field, after a short briefing, and experiment with it. The general argument for this method was that the schedule was too long and complicated to learn otherwise. This system threw a considerable strain on the field editor.

Problems of Comparability

The above detailed description is given for the purpose of indicating the extreme difficulty of securing unity in the Regional Office in the materials from the five states. Yet, under the plan of operating, such was necessary before the data could be tabulated. The work of editing would have been greatly simplified had the data from each state been tabulated separately. This would not have solved the problem however, since the aim of the regional study was to secure comparable data from the five states. Recognition of state difference in the usage of terms would probably have been more difficult to detect at a later stage than in the editing procedure. On the other hand, in some of the items, the divergence of interpretation between the states was so great that editing could not adjust the differences. In such cases the regional analysis takes cognizance of these differences.

All items tabulated under the same heading for the five states were made comparable by editing. All discrepancies were indicated. This meant that in the final analysis it was necessary in the Regional Office to translate all variations in language interpretation into uniform items. Frequently this necessitated the study of the schedules as individual cases. Measures of certain items are repeated in different forms as many as four times on the schedule. If the answers varied, the situation was determined for final tabulation on the basis of the context of the whole situation.

The task of editing the schedules before final tabulation therefore was exceedingly difficult. In brief the following items had to be taken into consideration: (1) differences in the mechanical set-up of each state schedule; (2) interpretation of each item; (3) expressed and real purpose of each question as differing between the states; (4) interpretation of enumerator; (5) adjustment for the time the schedule was taken; (6) how calculations were made; (7) differences in methods of editing and transcribing; (8) differences in various local settings of the information; (9) government programs operating in the area; (10) local prices, value of equipment and livestock, yields by specific crops, harvesting and marketing practices; (11) organization of the community to determine the eligibility of participation. In other words proper editing in the Regional Office presupposed a general knowledge of every area to which the schedule applied and specific knowledge about a great many items. In working out these details members of the regional staff were of course in constant touch with the various parts of the region.

PROBLEM OF WHAT TO TABULATE

Plan for First Worker's Conference

Although it had been decided that the work of tabulation was to be carried on in the Regional Office and that the state workers were to indicate the tabulations desired, the problem still remained of finding a satisfactory method of translating the desires of the tenure workers in the five states into some kind of instructions or procedures suitable to guide the tabulation work of the regional staff. With a simple body of information the tabulations to be made might have been more or less obvious. In the present instance, however, it became increasingly evident that the decisions relative to the detail of the tabulations constituted some of the most important decisions to be made in the project.

It may be suggested that the tabulations should have been determined at a much earlier stage in the project—at the time the research goals of the project were set up, or at latest, when the schedule was designed. The schedule designers of course had matters of tabulation in mind but they were at that time unable to visualize a great deal of the detail which would finally be available from these materials. It should be borne in mind that they were laboring with at least two combinations of data with which there was small precedent, that is, the combination of tabulations for the several subject matter fields of land economics, farm management, and rural sociology, and in addition the data from the several sections of the region. At any rate, without trying unduly to justify the procedure which was followed, it is only fair to state that many new combinations of data were evolved at the workers' conference which had not been anticipated before, and could not have been, since the experiences of these conferences went considerably beyond the previous thinking of the individual members or of the departments which they represented.

In order to cope with the problem the Regional Office drew up a plan suggesting that the state employees responsible for the actual work of the project in the states be brought together at the regional headquarters so that they might discuss and outline the tabulations that ought to be made from the data assembled in the Farm and Family survey. It was pointed out that this would also tend to orient the thinking of the project workers toward a common objective, facilitate the interpretation and analysis, and provide a basis for understanding how state interpretations would fit into the regional analysis.

At the Regional Committee meeting held in January, 1943, therefore, the Project Director presented the following plan which was unanimously adopted.

PROPOSED MEETING OF STATE WORKERS

Purpose of meeting

To discuss in detail plans for the tabulation and analysis of the data collected in the first phase of the intensive survey, that relating to the Farm and Family Schedule.

It is expected that at this meeting the group would (1) outline the tabulations of data which should be made from the regional schedule and (2) consider what portion of the analysis of the data should be done on a regional basis and what on a state basis only. The meeting would last at least ten days and be held as soon as a satisfactory time can be arranged.

Who would be expected to attend meeting

It is essential that each person attending this meeting has certain qualifications which permit him to make a distinct contribution to the discussion at the meeting and to take back to one of the states some ideas which will be helpful in carrying on the work to be done in that state. To qualify a person should: (1) be very familiar with the content, interpretations, etc., of the regional schedule and have had rather close contact with the field work on the project; (2) be a regular staff member who is in a position to give consideration to the analysis of the data from a research point of view (have background of research training and experience) and expect to provide much of the leadership in the state on the project during its entire lifetime.

In the meeting it will be assumed that the person, or persons, in attendance from a given state will serve as representatives of that state and be in position to indicate fully what the wishes of those in his state are on the matters under consideration.

Preparation of workers for meeting

In order that the meeting may be of the greatest possible value to all concerned, each person planning to attend is expected to do the following in advance of the meeting:

1. Confer with others in his state concerning what tabulations of the data should be made and how the analyses should be handled.

2. Prepare and submit to the Regional Office at least a week in advance of the meeting (in order that copies can be made for all persons in attendance), a *detailed* outline of his state's suggestions relative to tabulations and analyses. Specific instructions concerning the preparation of this outline will be sent at a later date direct to each person expected at the meeting.

The First Workers' Conference

The First Workers' Conference was held at the project headquarters in Fayetteville, Arkansas, March 23 to April 2, 1943.[1] This was the beginning of a series of workers' conferences and in fact the beginning of a new epoch in the project development. The opening remarks to the conference by the Project Director, which are reported in full in the conference minutes, were designed specifically to impress the conference members with the fact that the responsibility for carrying forward the work of the project fell directly upon their shoulders.

In order to facilitate the workings of the conference, each member had been asked to prepare an outline of his proposed tabulations of data in advance and to come to the conference thoroughly prepared to discuss the subjects under consideration. For the sake of uniformity in presentation, all information on the schedule was to be considered under one of twelve subject matter headings and a fairly definite procedure for indicating desired tabulations under each heading was established. These twelve headings were:

1. Leasing Arrangements
2. Ownership
3. Tenure Changes, Migration, and Mobility of Individual
4. Non-operating Owner
5. Use of Labor on Farm

1. Minutes First Workers' Conference, Regional Land Tenure Research Project, Fayetteville, March 23 to April 2, 1943, dittoed, 72 pp.

6. Credit Used
7. Farm Organization
8. Family Composition, Characteristics, and Health
9. Housing and Household Equipment
10. Social Participation
11. Participation in Public Programs
12. Changes in Farm Organization

After the opening remarks by the Project Director the group settled down to the task of planning the data tabulations. Each session of the Conference was presided over by a representative from one of the five states. Each of the eight state representatives served as chairman at least once.

Much of the spade work of the Conference was done by committees that met between the general sessions to work out especially knotty problems. The chairman of each committee was a state representative and the secretary, a member of the regional staff. All persons in attendance at the Conference were members of one or more committees and an effort was made to secure representation on each committee by all subject matter fields. The committee chairmen reported periodically to the whole group on the progress of their committee's deliberations and when definite decisions had been reached the matter was taken up and acted upon in one of the general sessions.

Organization of the First Workers' Conference

For this experiment in regional research a crucial period in subject matter cooperation came at the first workers' conference. The administrative problems in setting up the project had been numerous, but these problems were more or less by-products of the real task of the Project, that of actually coordinating the thinking of the tenure workers of the region so that their combined efforts would result in better and more economical work than could be accomplished without such regional effort. Up to this point, as has already been suggested, numerous mistakes had been made in co-ordinating the collection of the materials. But regardless of this past history, a group of interested tenure workers now faced a complex body of schedule data upon which they were desirous of combining their best efforts. To a number, research had previously constituted an individual procedure. The conference was now distinctly challenged with the problem of whether or not it could devise ways and means of tangibly objectifying the best thinking of the group. The ability to meet that challenge appeared to be dependent on not only the will to cooperate, but on working out the necessary details to facilitate efficient cooperation. The organizational set up of the conference therefore had been a subject of deep concern to the regional staff.

Since punch card machine tabulation had already been decided upon by the group, the immediate problems facing the conference had to do with the manner in which the data should be put on the punch cards. This involved deciding what was to be put on the cards as contrasted with hand tabulations, how it was to be put on, what materials were to go on what cards, and in general the types of statistical sorts that were wanted.

As already indicated, the subject matter had been broken down into twelve major fields and the members of the conference had already sent in brief statements of tabulations that they would desire in working out the materials in these fields. All of these suggestions had been dittoed and were passed out to the conference members so that the composite results of the suggestions were available. The conference then proceeded to add to and amend the suggestions that had been made. It was of course understood that the conference could not decide all details. In fact many decisions had to be made by the regional staff later—perhaps more than were made at the conference. Yet it was possible to get the general thinking of the conference members so that the direction of tabulation was determined.

To facilitate the conference discussion each of the 12 major subjects was set up on a separate ruled sheet with the so-called *control* items listed on the left and the *tabulated* items at the top as follows.

Leasing Arrangements	Value of perquisites	Degree of management	Type of landlord	Kinship to landlord	Gross farm income	Etc.	(Total of 41 items included in this list)
Tenure status							
Color							
Value of rental payment							
Degree of management							
Form of leasing agreement							
Etc.							

(Total of 13 items included in this list)

Setting up a tabular scheme of this kind of course left much to be desired in terms of giving the final answers to all sorts and tabulations that should be made. It was however a very valuable exercise and brought out the thinking of the group on the various problems. (1) It was possible with this scheme to indicate in general the items which were to be related to each other. (2) It tended to unify the terminology. (3) Terms which were not clear were defined. (4) The need for summary measures was indicated.

Much of the detailed work of the conference was done in smaller committees. Whenever problems came up which were not suitable for the larger group discussion they were referred to the appropriate committee and later reported back to the entire conference for confirmation or modification.

Most of the committee work was handled by three committees:

(1) Farm Tenure Status Committee (2) Farm Management Committee (3) Social Index Committee.

A stenographic record was kept of the conference, the results of which were made available to all concerned in dittoed form. (See previous citation.) In general the results of the conference were very satisfactory. The general feeling of the conference members was that they had been mutually helpful to each other in the task before them and that they had now gone beyond the area of simply talking cooperation into the realm of actual progress in the accomplishment of their scientific endeavors. The regional staff was given the necessary instruction so that it could proceed with the tabulations, knowing in general at least, what was wanted by the state workers. However, the task of excuting the desires of the conference was a complicated one to say the least, partly because many more tabulations had been suggested than could possibly be made, partly because of the extreme amount of detail involved and partly because, as already intimated, the state materials were not uniform in many respects.

Tabulation Procedure

The tabulation tasks in the Regional Office fell under the following headings:

1. Checking and editing. This work consumed a great amount of the time of the statistical and clerical workers in the Regional Office for at least a year after the first schedules came in. As long as coding was being done it was necessary to spend a considerable amount of time in checking and editing.

2. Making work sheets for extensions and computed factors to be coded. This task comprised such items as summation of sales, values, percentages of equity, various ratios, number of moves, years on present farm, value of rental payment, income summaries, value of farm investment, net worth, labor on farm, animal units on farm, land use and crop organization, production man units, man equivalent units, etc.

In addition to these computations it was necessary to compute various indices such as the crop yield index, the index of diversification, the socio-economic status index, migration index, stage of family cycle, degree of management index, and others. Some of these factors were rather readily computed whereas others involved a long process and as in the extreme case of socio-economic status the summation of a great number of schedule items. As the tabulation proceeded, however, the necessity of utilizing summary measures became increasingly evident and a great deal of time was spent on these computations. The necessity for the extended use of these measures was first brought to the attention of the group at the First Workers' Conference and as a result a special social index committee was appointed.

3. Preparing the Code. The preparation of codes to cover the situations in all of the states was a task of considerable complexity. In the first place very little could be done by way of developing a frequency distribution until the schedule material for the item in question had been gone over for all of the states rather carefully. Also since there were a great many people working at the task of coding it was necessary to have the details rather well crystallized before work commenced. Something over twenty items were repeated on most of the cards as control items. Since many of these were indices of summary measures of one kind or another a great deal of preparatory work had to be done before the first card was made up.

4. Coding. The data were coded on seventeen 80-column IBM (International Business Machine) cards. All codes were dittoed and sent to the state workers. The codes for these seventeen cards comprise a total of 261 dittoed pages. In a number of instances where the data from the five states varied greatly, as for example, Acres in Cropland as between Texas and Mississippi, a separate code was set up for each state.

5. Checking the Coding. This was of course a routine procedure but rather time-consuming.

6. Punching the Cards. Some difficulty was encountered in the employment of key punch operators. But in general this work proceeded with considerable dispatch once the tabulation sheets were ready for punching.

7. Verifying, Editing, and Correcting. The cards were put through regulation IBM tests in order to verify them before being run.

8. Making the IBM Machine Runs. This subject is discussed in some detail later in this report under the heading, "Returning Data to States."

9. Checking IBM Runs and Preparing Them to Send to the States. This subject is discussed in some detail later in this report under the heading, "Returning Data to States."

ITEMS OTHER THAN FARM AND FAMILY SCHEDULE
The Second Workers' Conference

The general setup of the second conference was similar to that of the first conference excepting that more of the work was carried on by the group as a whole rather than through committees. This was because of the nature of the subject matter rather than to any change in conference organization.

The general purpose of the Second Workers' Conference was that of considering details of study procedure relative to certain angles of the Project which were taken up only incidentally at the first conference. For the most part, these items are valuable to the Project in that they serve to give further illumination to problems already raised by the materials collected on the Farm and Family Schedules.

The agenda for the conference included the following subjects: The Farm Security Study, The Impact of the AAA Program on Tenure, The Institutional and Community Phases of Land Tenure, Potential Sources of Secondary and Supplementary Information, Farm Practice Sheets and Tenure Classification.

Preceding the conference a series of four memoranda were sent from the Regional Office to the tenure workers outlining the plan of the conference and requesting that certain materials be prepared in advance. These were included in the minutes of the conference.[2]

RETURNING DATA TO STATES
Plan of Work

The general plan of work for the project contemplated that both state and regional reports would be forthcoming from the cooperative work. Early in the history of the project it was emphasized that, "The intent of the Project is to facilitate and amplify the work within the individual state experiment stations and at the same time to develop a pooling of effort which will result in a regional product. It cannot be too strongly emphasized that the

2. Minutes Second Workers' Conference, Regional Land Tenure Research Project, Fayetteville, Arkansas, November 16-19, 1943, 129 pp. plus Appendix, dittoed.

regional product is dependent mainly on the work done in the states."[3]

Under this arrangement it was contemplated that while the regional report would necessarily be more than a compilation of state reports, it would rely heavily upon the analysis of information within the states for its contents. In discussing this general problem at the Memphis Committee Meeting (January, 1943) an extreme point of view taken by one member of the committee indicated that, "the regional report would be a summary of material from each of the states, and that there was no difference in the regional product and the state product. The regional product will be the total of the several states."[4]

Statements from other committee members indicated, however, that they did not hold this view, and the general viewpoint was that it would "be necessary to make some interpretations on a strictly regional basis."

Basic to the general plan of collaborative effort between the states and the Regional Office was the necessity of returning the tabulated materials to the states so that they could proceed in their analysis. To this end the regional staff spent most of its effort up until the latter part of 1945 at this task. That is to say, the first consideration was that of getting the tabulated data back to the states in the form that would be suitable for their purposes, being mindful at the same time that comparability in the data between the several states was necessary for purposes of the more purely regional analysis. However, as the time passed, and as personnel conditions in the state departments incident to the war indicated that the state reports would not be finished in time for use in the regional report, it was deemed desirable that the situation be reappraised with a view to pushing forward on the regional report with or without benefit of support from the state reports. Under the date of September 21, 1945, therefore, the Project Director wrote out a statement on the situation which was sent both to the tenure workers and to the committee members. The course of action indicated was officially approved at the November, 1945 committee meeting in Starkville, Mississippi. The statement follows:

3. Harold Hoffsommer, "Organization and Objectives of the Regional Land Tenure Research Project," *Journal of Farm Economics*, XXV (February, 1943), 250.

4. Minutes Southwestern Land Tenure Research Committee, Memphis, Tennessee, January, 1943, p. 13.

"The general plan of the Regional Land Tenure Research Project called for the major work of tabulation to be done in the Regional Office. This has now been accomplished and the statistical reports have been sent to the states. The remaining tabulations are concerned chiefly with special conditions within individual states and the special interests of individual state workers. It is therefore recommended that duplicate punch cards be made available to each state and that any further tabulations desired by the individual states be made by the states themselves, unless special arrangement is made with the Regional Office to do this work. This general procedure was anticipated in the original working plan, the suggestion for the shift at this juncture being dictated largely by the fact that essentially all tabulations common to the several states have now been completed.

"The general nature of the tabulations to be done at the Regional Office was determined at the First Workers' Conference held in Fayetteville in the latter part of March, 1943. Six months later a Second Workers' Conference was held for the purpose of developing certain study procedures which had not been covered in the first conference. In the interim, tabulations in the Regional Office were going ahead. A Third Workers' Conference was held in April, 1945 for the purpose of criticizing the general content and organization of the statistical reports being issued from the Regional Office. Finally a fourth conference was held in July, 1945 to refine further the methods of analyzing the data on the basis of the tabulations issued from the regional office. A period of more than two years, therefore, elapsed between the First Workers' Conference and the Fourth, during which the major attention of the regional staff was centered upon making tabulations in accordance with the suggestions of the state workers. Up to September 21, 1945, a total of 1,617 statistical reports were issued from the Regional Office to the several states. So far as can now be ascertained the statistical reports give rather a complete coverage of the data excepting for items which are peculiar to the individual states or to the interests of individual workers. Up to the point now reached there appears to have been an advantage in handling the tabulations of the group of states as a unit. In addition to the saving incident to combining the several states in one mechanical operation, the scope of tabulations for the individual states has been enriched and a regional uniformity otherwise impossible, has been attained. Theoretically it might be desirable for the Regional Office to extend these services to the several states even in the lines of their special interests. Under present circumstances, however, several factors appear to make it unwise in this instance:

"1. The volume of work orders coming from the five separate states would be more than the limited personnel of the Regional Office could accommodate since, in the nature of the requests, each state tabulation would have to be handled separately.

"2. Up to the present the major effort of the Regional Office has been expended in work on state tabulations and on the mechanics of getting the data in shape for interpretation. If the Regional Office is to complete a regional report in the allotted time, the direction of its efforts must necessarily be changed.

"3. It is believed that the statistical reports already issued to the states could, without further refinement, provide the necessary data for a rather complete series of bulletins in each of the states. In fact, so far as the Regional Office can ascertain, although some requests for additional reports are coming in, it appears that no one of the states has approached the full utilization of the reports already available.

"4. Finally, as a practical procedure, there is some question as to whether or not the state workers desire or are in position to construct work orders, which can be handled as satisfactorily in the Regional Office as in the state in question. Frequently a work order is built upon the result of a preceding tabulation. Hence it may be more convenient to work with the machine so that work directions may be determined a step at a time as the analysis advances. Furthermore many research workers proceed rather informally and find it difficult to plan so as to give much advance direction. This difficulty is inherent in the nature of the research work itself and is also conditioned to some extent by the attitudes of research workers in adjusting individualistic methods to a plan of group cooperation.

"For these various reasons it appears that the project has now reached the stage at which it would be advantageous for the individual states to take the responsibility of working out whatever additional tabulations they may desire. The Regional Office, will, of course, facilitate this work and cooperate with the individual states in so far as it can. The initial stage of such facilitation constitutes the punching of duplicate sets of cards. However, it is recommended that this should not be undertaken until it is ascertained whether or not the state in question desires the duplicate cards. The process of duplication does not offer any considerable obstacle since it is neither time consuming nor expensive. The Regional Office will need to retain a set of all cards punched until its report is finished. Even after that, it is possible that such regional materials should be kept intact as a unit for future work and reference. It should be pointed out that in addition to the statistical reports the individual states already have the Codes, Explanation of the Codes, and all other explanatory materials related to the tabulation of the data."

Method of Transmittal

Although it had been decided that the data were to be tabulated in the Regional Office and returned to the states, no method had been worked out showing the detail by which this was to be accomplished. It was originally contemplated that most of the machine tabulations would be done on a sorter. This would have necessitated typing the materials for transmittal to the states. The question then arose as to whether only the raw data should be sent or whether they would be more useful if they were worked up into tables. Several serious objections appeared with reference to making up the more or less finished tables. In the first place, it would involve more work than the regional staff would be able to do. Secondly, it would involve too much judgment on the part of the regional staff as to just what was wanted in the states and would not leave sufficient flexibility for the use of the data. Other methods were therefore canvassed.

After some experimentation, the use of a 405 IBM Accounting Machine was decided upon as constituting the best procedure. Under this arrangement, duplicate copies could be made for use in the Regional Office and a minimum of additional work was needed to make them intelligible to the state workers. It was necessary however to set up a fairly elaborate system in order to secure accuracy and avoid confusion particularly since the reports were all in code. This system is described in a memorandum to the state workers at the time the first statistical reports were sent out on July 10, 1944. It is herewith quoted in part:

"Your Regional Staff has spent considerable effort in devising a plan whereby the data tabulated in the Regional Office may be returned to the states in easily accessible and intelligible form.

"We believe that we have hit upon a method which embraces those qualities and also allows for a maximum of flexibility in the utilization of the data within the states. The present shipment of data is the first of a series of shipments which you are to receive within the next several months. All subsequent materials will be handled on the same pattern, so that it should be relatively easy to cumulate the data in a logical and systematic way. Also since you have an outline of the cards to be punched, you can follow the progress which is being made toward the completion of the tabulations.

"Under separate cover we are mailing the following items:[5]

"1. *Codes*—The binder entitled *Codes* includes:

(a) Summary of Code for Card X

(b) Code for Card X

As the other Codes are developed and these materials become available, they will be sent to you and may be bound in consecutive order in this binder.

"2. *Editing Procedure*—The binder entitled *Editing Procedure* includes the statements on *Editing* which have been written to date. More will follow and may be bound in this same volume.

"3. *Explanation of Codes*—This constitutes a 5 x 8 Card Index Tray with alphabetically arranged Subject Matter Guide Cards. These Guide Cards are keyed to the *Codes*. In looking over the Card X *Code* you will probably note various items which need explanation. If, for example, you note in Columns 32-33-34 "Cropland, *acres* in" and you wish to know how this was computed, you have only to turn to the Card File and look under Acres (the word underlined in the Code item in question) for the explanation. In other words, the Regional Office is attempting to make readily available an explanation of the basis upon which the Coding was done. Additional Guide Cards, or at least the subjects for them, will be sent you as the need for further explanations for the Codes arises. These Cards can then be inserted into the

5. See Appendix for samples of the following types of materials referred to below as they were sent from the Regional Office to the states: (1) Summary of Code (2) Code (3) Explanation of Codes (4) Description of Statistical Reports (5) Regional Table.

Card Index Tray so as to maintain the alphabetical sequence. You will note that the minor headings under the Guide Cards are also arranged alphabetically.

"4. *Reports*—These consist of tabulations from the 405 IBM Accounting Machine. These *Reports* are all being made in duplicate or triplicate, the original going to the State in question, the duplicate remaining in the Regional Office. All *Reports* will be identified in the right hand corner by the Card designation to which the *Report* applies, followed by consecutive numbers beginning with 1 and continuing through the entire list of *Reports* sent out. To each of the States of Arkansas, Mississippi, Oklahoma, and Texas, Reports 1, 2, 3, and 4 are being sent at this time.

"*Card X—Report No. 1* carries a penciled explanation of the manner in which this and subsequent *Reports* are to be read. There is also appended to this *Report* an explanatory statement. In order, so far as possible, to minimize error all *Reports* are being edited in the Regional Office before they are sent out. The *Reports* being sent at this time are only a part of those that you will receive on Card X. More will come later.

"We have tried to be as explicit as possible regarding the method by which the data are being submitted, but at best there are difficulties in an explanation of this kind. So far as we know there isn't much precedent to follow. Whatever is not clear, we shall be glad to attempt to clarify and whatever suggestions you have will be greatly appreciated."

The plan as indicated above was followed throughout the Project with good success. At the Third Workers' Conference which convened after the plan had been in operation for eight months, the system was appraised in some detail. The conference agreed that it was working satisfactorily and had no changes of consequence to suggest. The materials sent out unavoidably constituted a vast amount of detail and their translation into finished statistical tables required detailed planning and considerable work. In view of the research task, however, this work would have been much the same regardless of where the tabulations were run.

As the codes for each card were finished they were sent out to the state workers.

Since there were seventeen statistical cards, seventeen separate codes and summaries of codes were sent out.[6] These codes constituted the basis for the translation of all statistical reports.

As specialized interpretations of the tabulation procedure were worked out dittoed statements were issued to the tenure workers in a loose-leaf binder entitled *Editing Procedure*.[7] In its completed form this volume contained eleven articles or statements as follows:

(1) General Procedure for Editing Schedules. (2) Procedure Followed in Rounding Off Fractions and Use of the "x" Overpunch. (3) Method of Determining Score for Index of Management. (4) Procedure Followed in Editing Livestock Data. (5) Procedure Followed in Editing Tenure Status, Tenure Change, and Number of Moves. (6) Procedure for Editing Crop Organization and Land Use. (7) Credit. (8) The Family Socio-Economic Status Scale. (9) The Migration Index. (10) The Fertility Index. (11) Punch Card Procedure on Card B.

As already stated, the *Explanation of Codes* consists of a 5 x 8 Card Index Tray with subject matter guide cards keyed to the codes. This system worked admirably in that additional cards could be added as the work developed. At least 12 major guide cards representing new subjects were added after the cards were first issued. As finally completed the Explanation of Codes file contained a total of 42 guide cards and 344 subject matter cards. These cards contain the definitions of all important terms used in tabulating the data. Hence, interpretations in the state reports should be uniform and in accordance with the definitions used in the region as a whole. This dittoed file was sent to each tenure worker in the Region under the heading, *Explanation of Codes, Regional Land Tenure Research Project*.[8]

As to the statistical reports, a total of 2819 were sent to the states and an additional number were made up for special regional purposes. A duplicate of every report sent to the states was retained in the Regional Office. Also as these reports were sent out, a covering memorandum accompanied each shipment, stating in detail

6. See Appendix for sample code. The completed code books were dittoed under the title, *Codes*, Regional Land Tenure Research Project, Farm and Family Schedule, 261 pp.

7. Editing Procedure in the Regional Office for the Farm and Family Schedule, Regional Land Tenure Research Project, dittoed, 42 pp.

8. See Appendix for sample.

the content of the reports being sent.[9] Included also in each memorandum was a statement as to whether or not the shipment in question included the "final current installment" of the reports contemplated for the present on the given subject matter card which they covered. This made it possible for the state workers to request additional reports if the necessary materials for their purposes were not covered.

In addition to the above formal method of handling the data and its explanation, there was a considerable amount of personal correspondence, a number of visits between state and regional workers, either at the Regional Office or in one of the states, and finally the clearance through the workers' conferences.

Third Workers' Conference

Reference has already been made to the Third Workers' Conference.[10] After the plan for transmitting statistical data back to the states had been in operation for approximately eight months it was thought wise to confer, among other things, with respect to the problems involved in translating the statistical reports and to exchange techniques for handling the materials. The conference was therefore arranged to convene in Fayetteville in April of 1945.

Preceding the conference, the various members were advised as to the details to be considered and were given special assignments for reports and discussions in connection with the work that they had done and intended to do.

The objectives of the conference were as follows:

1. To take stock of what had been done on the Project in the States and in the Regional Office.

2. To study the technique of translating the statistical reports issued from the Regional Office into meaningful subject matter.

3. To determine the adequacy of the form and content of the statistical reports and to remedy their limitations wherever possible.

4. To devise better statistical methods for interpreting the Project data.

5. To consider the general content and organization of the proposed state and regional reports.

9. Volume entitled, Statistical Reports, Regional Land Tenure Research Project, dittoed, 50 pp, lists all statistical reports run. See Appendix for sample transmittal memoranda.

10. Minutes of the Third Workers' Conference, Regional Land Tenure Research Project, Fayetteville, Arkansas, April 10-12, 1945, dittoed, 111 pp. and Appendix.

6. To determine the methods and working arrangements in carrying the Project forward, which would best serve the interests of the individual states and the region as a whole.

The table of contents of the minutes of the Third Workers' Conference covers the following items: Progress Reports (from each state and regional worker); The Technique of Table Construction from Statistical Reports; Adequacy of Content of Statistical Reports for State and Regional Use; Statistical Problems in Relating Tenure Factors; Analysis of Size of Business; Number and Nature of State and Regional Reports Planned; Relation Between State and Regional Data. The Appendix includes the following: Key Words Used in Proposed State Report Statements; Proposed State Reports.

CHAPTER FIVE

Writing The Reports

THE STATE REPORTS PLANNED

At the outset of the Project it was assumed that there would be both state and regional reports issuing from the data collected. Although doubtless the tenure workers had a fairly definite conception of what these reports would contain since they were limited largely by the available survey data, no definite report outlines were developed for submission to the project until September, 1943. At the regional committee meeting convening in St. Louis at this time, the committee members were asked to submit brief statements of the titles and the content of each report that they hoped to develop in their states. The statements submitted were in most cases planned by those who intended to do the actual work although it was later discovered in a workers' conference that in several cases the workers in question were not familiar with the outline which the committee member had presented from his state. Under such a situation it was highly questionable of course whether or not the report as outlined would be followed out. In most cases the contemplated work was considerably larger than that actually accomplished. One reason for this was obviously that the department members were simply not available to do the work as had been anticipated. Another was that the work turned out to be more complex than was expected.

In the following June, 1944 at the Dallas committee meeting, the Regional Committee members were asked to revise their previous statements in the light of the current conditions. A compilation of these two statements together with comments by the tenure workers on these statements is found in the Third Workers' Conference Minutes.[1]

1. Minutes Third Workers' Conference, Regional Land Tenure Research Project, Appendix, pp. 1-9. Comments by the tenure workers with respect to these statements are found on pages 83 to 87.

In general the trend of comment by the tenure workers was to the effect that it would be difficult to work out all that had been outlined. Also, in several instances, due to turnover of personnel, the emphasis of the reports was to be altered somewhat.

A brief statement of the bulletins planned by the several states follows:

Arkansas

1. Trends in Tenure in the Delta, Coastal Plain, and Hilly Upland, 1932-1941

2. Agricultural Production and Efficiency of the Individual Farm as Affected by Tenure (Coastal Plain)

3. Landlord-Tenant Contracts and Relations (Coastal Plain)

4. Rural Institutions, Social Habits, and Participation as Affected by Tenure (Coastal Plain)

5. Characteristics and Performance of FSA Clients as Compared with Comparable Groups of Non-Clients (Coastal Plain)

6. Legal Aspects of Land Tenure in Arkansas

7. Agricultural Production and Efficiency on Individual Farms as Affected by Tenure in Boone County (Ozark Region)

8. Social and Community Participation in Boone County (Ozark Region)

The reports referred to under numbers 1, 6, 7, and 8 above are not a part of the uniform five-state data but are closely related to it, some of the tabulations having been done in the Regional Office.

Louisiana

(Due to loss of personnel no definite publication plans were made.)

Mississippi

1. Land Tenure in the Upper Coastal Plain in Mississippi

2. Farm Organization and Operation in Upper Coastal Plains, Mississippi

3. Summary Reports in Mississippi Farm Research

a. Tenure Study in Mississippi

b. The Farm Security Program

c. Farm Management

Oklahoma (Rural Sociology)

1. Village Survey in Southwestern Oklahoma

2. Household and Family Composition
3. Housing Conditions in Relation to Tenure Economic status
4. Methods of Attaining Ownership
5. Mobility of Farm Operators
6. Patterns of Family Participation in Community Activities
7. Socio-Economic Factors in Tenure Status
8. Possible Miscellaneous Studies
   a. Sociological Aspects of Farm Labor Organization
   b. Sociological Aspects of Leasing Arrangements
   c. Health and Medical Service in Relation to Tenure and Economic Status

Oklahoma, Cont. (Agricultural Economics)
1. Land Tenure as Related to Farm Adjustments
2. Landlord-Tenant Business Relations—A Study Involving Types of Agreements
3. Farm Business Analysis—A Study of Farm Practices and Types of Farms in Relation to Tenure
4. Farm Finance, Sources of Credit and Methods of Use in Relation to Tenure
5. Land Ownership—A Historical Analysis Including the Methods of Land Acquisition and Present Status
6. Public Finance, Taxing Problems, Public Institutions, and Marketing Facilities
7. Irrigation Problems and Tenure Adjustments

It was expected when these reports were outlined that the Departments of Rural Sociology and Agricultural Economics would collaborate in writing certain of them.

Texas
1. Historical Trend Study
2. Legal Aspects of Farm Tenure
3. Efficiency of Labor Utilization in Relation to Tenure and Size of Farm
4. Farm Management Aspects of Land Tenure
5. The Social Aspects of Land Tenure
6. Mutual Aid Between Landlord and Tenant
7. The Economic Significance of Tenure in the Black Prairie
8. Production Requirements in Relation to Tenure
9. Social Participation in Relation to Tenure

BUREAU OF AGRICULTURAL ECONOMICS COOPERATION

From the beginning of the Project planning a member of the Division of Land Economics, Bureau of Agricultural Economics, served as a member of the Regional Committee. After the funds for the Project had been granted (the Bureau pledged a substantial amount of cooperation, largely in personnel), the question of the best method of Bureau cooperation was discussed at some length at the College Station, Texas, Regional Committee Meeting in July of 1942. The Bureau representative on the committee indicated that those he represented wished to furnish a full time man and felt that perhaps their greatest contribution might be on certain aspects "that would cut across state lines, rather than by furnishing additional field help or additional clerks or stenographers."

The Bureau representative then analyzed the phases of the study that might be a part of the contribution of the Regional Office of the Bureau and divided them into ten fields:

1. Historical analysis, using census and other historical records
2. Type-of-tenancy area studies
3. Legal aspects of land tenure
4. Homestead exemption
5. Effects of taxation on tenure
6. Foreign aspects
7. Land prices
8. Land policies
9. New ground settlement
10. General statistical compilations

A substantial part of the support indicated to the Project by the Bureau concerned statistical tabulations that were to be done by the Philadelphia Works Progress Administration project. This project was discontinued however before any of this work could be accomplished.

Unfortunately, because of calls to military service, the Bureau staff was badly depleted and the program could not be carried out in total. Generally speaking, however, the legal studies went on and rather late in the Project other personnel became available so that aid was given particularly in special phases of the final regional manuscript. The Bureau did not help at any stage of the project in the detail of the intensive survey but rather gave its support to the Project by collaborating in carrying out regional studies of a tenure nature which it already had under way. It also furnished a considerable amount of the equipment used in the Regional Office in the form of desks, typewriters and calculating machines, ditto machine, and other equipment at a time when the Project would have had great difficulty in securing these materials elsewhere because of the war situation.

REGIONAL REPORT PLAN

Although it had been generally understood from the beginning of the Project that there was to be a regional report, it was not until the November, 1945 Regional Committee Meeting at Starkville, Mississippi, after the Project had been in operation more than three years, that the regional staff was given official authority to proceed on such a report. In this, as with some of the other committee activities, the functions of the Regional Committee, as contrasted with those of the regional staff and the tenure workers, had not been clearly defined.

Even though official action on the matter of assigning the regional staff to write the regional report did not come until late in the Project the regional staff had previously spent a considerable amount of time in setting up procedures, which it was presumed would culminate in a regional report. In fact, it would have been impossible to have set up the detailed tabulations had there not been a fairly clear anticipation of the general nature of the report that was to follow. Working outlines had therefore been set up in the Regional Office early in the Project. One of these has already been indicated in the division of the tenure materials into twelve major divisions for the work of the First Workers' Conference.

Another question with respect to the regional report concerned not its detailed outline but its general viewpoint. Although there was some sentiment in the committee that the report should make pronouncements on policy it was generally accepted from early in the project work that such was not the major function of the undertaking. The essence of the study was conceived to be that of establishing relationships. Once these were established, the social planner could then make use of them for whatever purposes he might have in mind. Early in the Project the following statement on this subject was issued:

"In brief compass, the objective of the project is to relate land tenure status to farm family economic and social performance. In attaining this objective a fundamental problem is that of determining the criteria for classifying tenures into meaningful categories . . . Once the connection between tenure status and performance is made clear it will be possible to select the type of tenures which will aid in achieving the desired goals—whatever they may be—for farm life."[2]

Realizing however that the general end of all social science is social welfare, the Regional Committee considered that a policy statement should be made, based on the findings of the relationships established in the tenure report. At the time of this writing this report is being prepared by the Committee for publication apart from the larger tenure report.

As already indicated, regional report outlines were developed early in the Project. In fact, it may be said that the main chapter divisions of such a report were developed when the regional schedule was separated into its several major headings. Later more detailed outlines were developed, several of which were submitted to the Regional Office by state tenure workers and several members of the regional staff. These were formulated into a general outline, revised several times and finally presented to the Regional Committee as the third draft of the regional report outline at the above mentioned committee meeting in Starkville. Several suggestions were made at this time by the Committee and others with a fourth draft of the chapter outline resulting which is herewith reproduced.

THE SOCIAL AND ECONOMIC SIGNIFICANCE OF LAND TENURE IN THE
SOUTH CENTRAL STATES

A Report of the Findings of the Regional Land Tenure Research
Project (Summary Outline)

I. Introduction
II. The Classification of Tenure Types
III. General Characteristics of Farming and Farm Family Living in the Region
IV. Tenure and the Farm Business
V. Tenure and the Farm Family
VI. Tenure Change

2. Harold Hoffsomer, "Organization and Objectives of the Regional Land Tenure Research Project," *Journal of Farm Economics*, Vol. XXV (February, 1943), 256-57.

VII. Landlord Tenant Relations and Leasing Arrangements
VIII. Soil Conservation and Improved Farm Practices in Relation to Tenure
IX. Scale of Operation and Farm Tenure
X. Legal Aspects of Farm Tenure
XI. Use of Capital
XII. Farm Laborers and Mechanization
XIII. Government Programs and Farm Tenure
XIV. Community and Institutional Factors in Tenure
XV. Persistent Problems in Agriculture and Their Tenure Implications
XVI. Summary and Conclusions

Detailed outlines for the above chapter headings were worked out by the person or persons responsible for the writing with the collaboration of the entire regional staff. Since no fewer than eight persons worked on the report simultaneously and utilized much the same materials it became necessary to proceed very methodically to avoid confusion and duplication.

In the first place, it was obviously necessary to delimit the scope of the subject matter to be covered by each person. This was more or less automatically decided by previous interests and work on the project. It was hoped that some of the tenure workers in the states might be able to contribute specifically to the regional analysis in addition to their state work. This proved impossible, however, since under the general working arrangement the first duties of the state workers revolved around the production of state products, which were yet far from complete as the regional report was being finished. The personnel available therefore for writing the regional report was limited almost entirely to the regional staff members.

Drawing in personnel from the states to work on certain specialized phases of the regional report had been a concern since early in the Project. However, as the Project was organized, the state workers were preoccupied with their state reports so that the writing of the regional report was left largely to the regional staff. In retrospect it appears that greater cooperation in this matter might have been elicited from the state workers had they been formed into technical subcommittees to work on individual chapters of the regional report, probably under the chairmanship of a regional staff member. These reports might then have been published individually as experiment state bulletins or combined into book form. In some instances these subcommittees might well have been using these materials for theses for advanced degrees.

Despite the limited amount that the state workers were actually able to work on the regional materials as such, it is interesting to note that at a later committee meeting, when the Regional Committee was considering the advisability of beginning another regional project, one of the major arguments for so doing concerned the training which the members of the departments had received from the Regional Project association. Several members of the Committee alleged that certain members of their departments had been "made" as a result of the training they had received.

In working ahead on the regional report, each writer was asked to make a detailed outline of what he intended to cover. These outlines were then considered and criticized by all other members of the staff. In proceeding with this process, however, it was found that outlines alone did not give an adequate conception to other staff members as to just what was being covered. In other words, the abbreviated terminology of the outlines did not give an adequate conception of the direction of thinking and the particular aspect of the item mentioned that was to be discussed. Therefore, to these outlines, each writer was requested to write an introductory statement indicating his point of view. These statements proved to be very helpful in coordinating the work of the several writers. All of these materials were cleared through the Project Director. Several of the writers remained in the Regional Office only part time during the compilation of the report. In these instances they were furnished with new tables as they came out and otherwise kept in touch with the general progress of the work. They were also furnished with specific additional tabulations on request.

FOCAL POINTS OF ANALYSIS

The Third Workers' Conference concentrated largely on methods by which the data of the project could be most advantageously handled. At the time of this conference it was therefore contemplated that a fourth conference should be held at a later date, after the workers had had additional time to study the statistical reports which had been sent their states, for the purpose of dealing with the focal points of the subject matter itself. While it is true that the focal points in the study had been a matter of common discussion since the beginning of the Project it was found that there was a considerable difference of opinion after the analysis had got under way as to the priorities which the various phases of the data should assume. This problem became particularly pertinent in view of the complexity of the data and the varied interpretations as to the significant aspects within the field of tenure itself.

In order therefore to get the best possible coordination among the subject matter fields, the several states, and the Regional Office, a fourth conference was called to meet at the project headquarters in Fayetteville in July of 1945.[3]

To indicate the procedure used at this conference several memoranda prepared by the Project Director were sent to the tenure workers, the first of which is herewith quoted at some length.

"The Third Regional Land Tenure Research Workers' Conference requested me as Project Director to outline a plan of preparation for the Fourth Conference, to be held in Fayetteville beginning July 16, 1945.

"I assume that the basic element in such a plan concerns the arrangement of practical measures whereby the members of the conference may attain the best possible 'meeting of minds' on the subject matter in question. The Fourth Conference is not a substitute for the preparation of individual state manuscripts but is designed to convene at such a time as to lend maximum aid to the individuals whose responsibility it is to prepare such manuscripts. Each individual can therefore regard the conference as a sort of electrical 'boosting up' station along the line of his particular endeavor.

"To be effective, the conference must assume thorough familiarity with the data by those in attendance. This does not mean that the work will have reached manuscript stage by conference time, but it does imply that the various outlines of analyses will have been pretty well planned, and the supporting statistical data organized in understandable shape. To some individuals it may also mean fairly elaborate explanatory notes.

"By way of reiterating the expression of the Third Conference, it is agreed, I believe, that the emphasis in the forthcoming con-

3. Minutes of the Fourth Workers' Conference, July 16-20, 1945, Regional Land Tenure Research Project, dittoed, 53 pp.

ference should be strictly on *subject matter* as contrasted with the emphasis in the Third Conference on *method*. In other words, the appropriate preface to statements in this conference should be, 'Regarding the point under discussion, our data show, etc. etc.' It is likewise understood that the subject of land tenure should serve as the basic orientation for all discussion.

"A further consideration concerns delimiting the subject matter of the conference. The understanding in this regard is, I believe, that the conference effort is to center on the materials included on Cards 1 to 5 inclusive. (Household/Family Member; Farm Business and Labor; Land Use and Crop Organization; Income; Feed, Livestock and Credit.) This subject matter limitation is not intended to exclude data covered on other cards or data not on cards at all, for that matter. On the other hand it is recognized that in the relatively short time before the Fourth Conference, not all phases of the subject matter can be prepared satisfactorily for the purposes at hand. No one need feel inhibited, however, if he finds it possible to go beyond the marks set.

"In order to assure the desired 'meeting of minds,' I believe that it is necessary that certain focal points of interest be selected in advance, around which to center the preparation and the conference discussions. These focal points should be the ones which each person would normally select in proceeding with his analysis. Excepting for differences in emphasis, probably they will be pretty much the same for all workers. As the discussion of a given focal point proceeds, each individual should be able to fit his particular slant of the subject into the pattern of analysis. That is to say, these so-called focal points will expand and increase in complexity from relatively simple concepts to complex patterns of relationships which will tend to include the varying shades of emphasis and interest of the different members of the group.

"As I visualize it, the discussion procedure at the conference after the focal points have been chosen, should consist of three broad steps. Using *migration* as an example focal point, the first step would be to list under it the various hypotheses concerning the relation of migration to tenure.

"The second step would seek to determine whether or not the data are available to prove or disprove these various hypotheses. The hypotheses would probably fall into three classes, (a) those for which significant data are available from the regional project; (b) those for which significant data are available but not from the regional project; (c) those for which no significant data are now available anywhere. In (b), the citations should be listed and their uses indicated. In the case of (c), the hypotheses should be catalogued for use in future research.

"The third step would consist in citing regional data to prove or disprove the hypothesis in question. This would involve showing the statistical and other techniques by which the results were obtained. As a practical procedure, it would probably be desirable to key the data in some way to the statistical report from which they were taken, in order that others wishing to follow the same procedure may do so with a minimum of effort.

"It is obvious of course, that methods of handling the data, even to prove identical assumptions, will vary with individuals. In some instances any one of several methods may be equally effective, whereas in others a comparison of methods will reveal a superiority of one over the other. Furthermore, some of the workers may wish to refine their data more than others. For example, the crude data may show that tenants move more frequently than owners. This may be regarded as conclusive evidence by some and not by others. Some may wish to refine the data and will raise questions as to the influence of age, tenure of parents, size of farm, type of farming, community customs, credit facilities, outside employment, size of family, crops and other factors which they consider to be significant.

"Differences of opinion may be expected in all of the three steps noted above, but with the attention centered on specific items and supported by specific data, the discussions should hold definite values for every one. Such values would include (1) interchange of ideas with respect to focal points and their proper emphasis in tenure study; (2) interchange of hypotheses; (3) stimulation in the selection of suitable hypotheses for testing in individual states and according to individual interests; (4) interchange of methods of analysis; (5) revision of old and acceptance of new analytical procedures.

"An additional point may be mentioned with respect to the relation of the subject matter fields of Farm Management, Land Economics and Rural Sociology in the conference procedure described above. Tenure study indicates that the relationships of the various tenure factors continually cross and recross these subject matter lines. Hence, although the focal point under discussion may not be regarded as of primary interest in one or more of these fields, yet because of the inter-relationships of tenure factors, it is difficult to conceive of a focal point of interest which does not have its ramifications in all three of them. Thus, in the example given above, migration, though not a primary point of research in the field of Farm Management, yet holds definite interest for the farm management worker in relation to land tenure. Likewise, the rural sociology worker, though not ordinarily concerned with specific factors of farm organization, finds a knowledge of these factors indispensable in carrying forward the analysis of certain tenure-related social factors. It would seem, therefore, that differences in the focal points of interest between the three fields may be more largely a matter of emphasis on given points rather than in the identity of the points themselves."

In addition to the above general statement, a set of suggestions was sent to each tenure worker covering specific items upon which the conference members were to prepare in advance of the conference. Largely because of emergency factors brought on by World War II it was impossible for the conference members to devote as much time as might have been expected to preparation. These directions however did serve to center the thinking of the members so that when they came together there was substantial agreement as to what was to be done.

At the outset the conference[4] directed its attention to determining a method whereby it could utilize in the best manner the thinking of the group in centering upon the focal points of interest and in breaking these points down into sub-points for analysis. Considerable experimentation in method ensued but it was finally decided to go through the code book, determine the various "blocks" of data and develop suitable hypotheses for each. At the beginning it was thought wise to list the sub-propositions under each hypothesis as it was decided to develop the major hypotheses for the entire subject matter field and then to develop the detail for each of them.

4. Minutes Fourth Workers' Conference, Fayetteville, Arkansas, Regional Land Tenure Research Project, pp. 4, 6, 7, and 15 from which the following comments are summarized.

Having decided upon the major hypotheses the conference then wrestled further with the development of a suitable method for breaking them down into sub-propositions for analysis. The method of statement finally evolved nineteen hypotheses with sub-points for detailed analysis. In the case of the first four hypotheses the entire group working together formulated the statements. After this experience, however, it was deemed wise to break up into committees for this work. Accordingly the fourteen members were divided into seven committees of two each and each committee was assigned one major hypothesis at a time to report back to the entire group. The results of the sub-committee effort were then written on the board and revised by the entire group. In some instances the sub-committee revised the wording of the major hypotheses but this was usually done only if the original wording was obscure or covered too broad a scope.

For the purpose of getting the materials before the conference for discussion and decision the following scheme of presentation was used on a blackboard. An example of one of the hypotheses with explanations follows.

HYPOTHESIS VIII

The tenure arrangements under which a farm is operated are related to the socio-economic status of the farm family in question.

Controlled Conditions	First Term	Second Term	Sub-Propositions
1. Color	A. Tenure class	a. Socio-econ.	A-a
2. Family cycle	B. Farm Security	index score	B-b
3. Income	Administration	b. Housing	A-b, c
4. Size of farm	C. Kinship to landlord	c. Household	A-d
5. Value of farm		and cultural	A-e
property owned		possessions	etc.
6. Education		d. Participation	
		e. Stratification	

In the above scheme the column headed *Controlled Conditions* comprises those items which must be watched if the analysis of the hypothesis is to be valid. In many instances these amount to underlying factors which would upset all other analyses of the point if they were not taken into consideration. As the title and function of the column was being developed, it was several times referred to as the "Beware" column. These items, of course, vary for the different hypotheses.

In general the *First Term* as indicated in most of the hypotheses refers to some type of tenure arrangement, the most common of which was "Conventional Classification." This signifies the tenfold classification of Full Owner, Part Owner, Indeterminate Tenure, etc., as listed in the code. However, since this is not a valid classification for all purposes other classifications or sorts were suggested in this column to take the place of the conventional classes. For example, in Hypothesis II "equity" and "index of management" were indicated as sorts to be used in lieu of the conventional classes.

The column *Second Term* refers to the second focal term used in the hypothesis and in general shows a method by which the item in question may be sorted or measured. For example, in Hypothesis II, the "second term" is "land use." Several methods for measuring land use are indicated, beginning with "diversification index" and ending with "physical volume of production."

Sub-Propositions. This column refers to the manner in which the items under "First Term" and "Second Term" are to be related. For example, in Hypothesis VIII, the first entry in this column is A-a. This means that some relation is to be established between the conventional tenure classes and socio-economic status. Since there are ten conventional tenure classes indicated in the code the possibilities of comparisons on this particular point are rather numerous. A general method of stating A-a, which would need further breakdown for analysis, would be, "The type of tenure class to which a farmer belongs is related to his socio-economic status." In such a statement the socio-economic status may be conceived to be fundamental in influencing the tenure status, or turned the other way around, the tenure status may be thought to be influential in determining the socio-economic status. No indication is given as to which is assumed to be more important. This sub-proposition, as above stated, is in a general form and needs to be broken down for purposes of testing. Yet the nature of this testing is implied. The general sub-proposition when divided into smaller propositions may be stated either in the form of a regular hypothesis or in the form of a question as, "Full owners have a higher socio-economic status than share renters," or "Do owners have a higher socio-economic status than tenants?" The proposition might also be translated into the "if then" formulation.

Since the beginning of the project the unwieldiness of the subject had been a matter of considerable concern. This, added to the attempt to coordinate several subject matter fields in a region with wide variation, proved to be a baffling problem. It was particularly disconcerting to new workers who came on the project. They were greatly perplexed as to how to attack the great mass of assembled information. The Fourth Conference cleared up a great deal of these orientation difficulties. In general the tenure workers left the conference with a much clearer view as to how they might best proceed with their reports. Unfortunately, most of the state members of the group were unable to work consistently on the tenure materials because of other duties.

THE FIFTH WORKERS' CONFERENCE

Up until shortly before this conference the emphasis in the activity of the Regional Office had been that of furnishing tabulations to the several states for their use in writing state reports. This work was now largely completed and with the end of the project period approaching the regional staff turned its effort to assembling the data for the regional report. This proved to be a greater task than had been anticipated. The advisability of adding together the data for the several states to form a total or average needed to be considered more or less separately for each individual point. The members of the regional staff were in some disagreement over some of the items. Moreover, the computation of relatives and other statistical indexes so as to make the state data comparable constituted a time-consuming task.

The general purpose of the Fifth Conference was to present for critical evaluation the tentative conclusions from the manuscripts under way in the states, and also to discuss some of the procedures being used in regional analysis. The nature of the materials presented is indicated in connection with the individual reports in the body of the conference minutes.[5]

The agenda for the conference was organized in advance. State tenure workers were chairmen of the sessions in which the conclusions and observations of the other tenure workers were submitted. In addition, these chairmen were made responsible, in part, for writing up the minutes of the sessions over which they presided.

The conference was limited by the fact that not all of the state

5. Minutes Fifth Workers' Conference, Fayetteville, Arkansas, December 11-14, 1945, dittoed, 28 pp., and Appendix including 10 regional statistical tables.

workers were prepared to report effectively on their data and to achieve thus fully the objectives of the meeting. Of the five states represented, only two had gone far enough to draw significant conclusions from their intensive survey data. In these two states only a fraction of the data had been covered. In a third state, several studies were presented which were related to the regional study but which were not a part of the intensive survey common to the five states. The latter part of the conference was taken up with a discussion of regional materials based on a series of dittoed regional tables which were made available to the conference members.

Lack of preparation for this conference may be ascribed largely to the wartime emergency conditions which existed during the time the Project was under way. In not a single state of the five was a project leader able to function continuously throughout the Project. In several of the states there were several changes back and forth. For example, in one state the regular tenure man in the department began the work. Well started, he was called to military service and another man substituted. The second man served long enough to get well into the project work but resigned his position to accept government work. A third man was employed. Not being a specialist in the field and coming into the Project at a time when the procedures were well advanced he was at a great disadvantage. He continued the work however until near the end of the Project when the original and permanent man in the department, after an absence of several years, came back. This state was intensely interested in the project work and cooperated in every possible way but was obviously operating under unusual handicaps because of the war emergency. In this state the regional materials will be used extensively but actually several years were lost due to personnel turnover.

It should be further pointed out that in certain types of work turnover of personnel would not be so serious. But in the necessarily complex structure necessary to the functioning of a project of this kind, turnover of personnel could not but have serious effects. Furthermore, just as the work was settling down in several of the states and it was hoped that progress could be made on the tenure reports, the influx of veterans into the schools took place, necessitating rearranged schedules and in some instances taking men almost entirely out of research to fill the unusual demand for teachers.

Without question the excessive turnover of state personnel was one of the most serious obstacles faced by the Project. In the one instance in the region in which a state tenure worker maintained the same status in the tenure work of his state from the beginning to the end of the project, this person produced three printed experiment station bulletins besides other project materials during the four-year course of the Project. It is entirely possible, of course, that from the point of view of state publications, the effect of the turnover of personnel was more that of slowing up the issue of the publications rather than reducing their number. The next several years will yield evidence in this regard.

This retardation in state work meant that the state analyses were almost completely lost to the regional report, which was necessarily obliged to meet the deadline of the project termination. Although it seemed at the time of writing the regional report that the lack of completed state reports was a decided handicap it is doubtful whether from the standpoint of the total information to be yielded by the Project this constituted as grave a limitation as then appeared. In the first place, the regional report could not contain the amount of detail that might be utilized in a state report. Therefore, even though the state reports had been available it is probable that their use in the regional manuscript would have been limited. Furthermore, materials of this nature which would have been included in the regional report will be included in the state reports anyway. In addition, since many of the regional materials, which are simply the state materials used in combination, were available to the state writers, they were used to advantage in developing the state manuscripts.[6] Probably of most importance, however, is the fact that although the regional manuscript could not draw on state manuscripts to any great extent, the state workers actually *were* cooperators in the preparation of the regional manuscript through the workers' conferences and other contacts incident to the regional work. The Sixth Workers' Conference[7] was devoted almost exclusively to the regional report. Extensive revisions and additions resulted. It is entirely probable that this type of cooperation was the most effective that could have been achieved.

6. See Appendix for list of published state reports.
7. Minutes Sixth Workers' Conference, Fayetteville, Arkansas, June 25-28, 1946, dittoed, 8 pp.

CHAPTER SIX

Administrative Arrangements

Some of the conditions relating to the selection of a headquarters location were given above under the title of "Project Organization." Another condition that should be mentioned is the fact that the General Education Board made its grant of funds "to the University of Arkansas toward support during the three year period . . . of land tenure studies by the Southwestern Land Tenure Research Committee, expenditures to be made on order of the Committee."[1] As a result, the University felt a responsibility for the funds and in meeting this responsibility considered, at the beginning at least, the funds subject to the same regulations as other funds disbursed by the institution. This fact no doubt contributed to several points of misunderstanding to be mentioned.

Before the headquarters was selected committee members canvassed the possibilities in their various states, particularly with respect to whether or not the colleges in question would be able and willing to act as a disbursing agent for the funds. From the reports back to the committee it appears that this probably could have been arranged in any of the states. In fact the school administrations and their business offices showed a definite interest in cooperating with the project. Although the Committee voted, seeing no other satisfactory solution, to have one of the colleges handle the project funds, there was a certain skepticism as to how it would work out. The minutes at the time of this decision carry the following comment:

"The consensus of opinion seemed to be that it would be more

1. Quoted from a letter of February 27, 1942 received by President A. M. Harding, University of Arkansas, from Fred McCuistion, Acting Secretary of the General Education Board.

desirable to operate as an independent agency if possible. Various members of the Committee pointed out that it was their understanding that the University was to serve only as the fiscal agent of the Committee; and that the Committee would not need to operate under the state regulations, but would operate under regulations which it would establish. Most of the Committee members felt that if the University regulations were applied to the regional staff, the use of funds would be less flexible and it would be more difficult to operate within the five states without a great deal of red tape.

"The Committee felt that even though the University took the responsibility of making the appointments, it would still be necessary for the Project Director and the representative of the Committee to check that the funds were expended according to the wishes of the Committee and for the purpose for which they were appropriated."

The experience of the Project indicates the necessity for very careful procedure at this point. In discussing the requisites of a disbursing agency members of the Committee were concerned on a number of specific points: (1) Would the University in any way interfere with the flexibility of the project procedures? (2) Would the Committee be free to make appointments as it saw fit? (3) Would the University accept the recommended salaries without question? (4) On what basis would expenses be handled? (5) What would be the cost to the Project for such service?

These questions were presumably answered in a satisfactory manner. Actually, however, it was not until the project headquarters was moved from the University campus to a private building nearly a year after the beginning of the Project that the problems suggested by these questions were adjusted. But in the main the difficulties experienced resulted from a lack of advance detailed knowledge of just what the Project problems as related to the University would be.

At the outset of the Project the status on the University campus of the members of the regional professional and office personnel was not clear. A source of confusion in the situation was that the Committee itself had not made a definite pronouncement as to its wishes in the matter, although it had been much discussed. There was a considerable sentiment that if the regional staff became regular members of the University staff, it would be too much dominated by the rules and regulations of the University, whereas actually it was regionally employed and obligated to the other four states equally as much as to the state in which the headquarters happened to be located. The problem of maintaining the necessary regional identity and at the same time being members of one of the cooperating state staffs proved a difficult balance for the regional staff to achieve. The method of handling the funds made the regional employees "official" members of the University staff and they were welcomed as such by the regular University staff members. This made for a pleasant personal relationship for regional staff members. It was thought best however to emphasize as much as possible the regional aspects of the work by the use of a regional project letterhead, regional expense forms, and the like, so that the emphasis would not appear to be too much on the headquarters University.

Numerous minor questions arose at the beginning of the Project and bobbed up occasionally throughout, particularly with regard to the secretarial and clerical workers. Were the regional employees, for example, eligible for the University insurance plan? Should the clerical workers be subject to the University rating scale and required to take the tests prescribed for regular University employees? Should salary checks be held up until the state poll tax had been paid? Such minor problems were all finally adjusted satisfactorily but would have caused much less friction had they been more adequately anticipated.

Another type of problem that gave rise to a certain amount of friction concerned the handling of expense accounts. All expense accounts cleared through the University business office. No two of the schools in the region had the same expense account regulations, hence many adjustments in procedure were necessary. Since the headquarters University handled the accounts from all of the states and since it was desirable that its routine be disturbed as little as possible in so doing, regional project expense account regulations were set up to conform as nearly as possible with the established procedure of the University. A regional expense form with appropriate instructions was designed for use whenever regional funds were involved. This worked reasonably well except that the Regional Office had a good deal of editing of accounts, particularly at the beginning, since the detail of the regional procedure necessarily varied from the customary practices, particularly in the states other than the headquarters state.

Some of the more persistent nuisances in this regard concerned variation between the states as to items for which expense would be allowed, such as tips, car storage, and limitation on price of meals. Also, certain regulations while workable on a state basis, became unwieldy and impractical when applied to the region. One such regulation, later abandoned, necessitated that a travel requisition be issued in advance by the Regional Office for individual trips, or at least as often as each two weeks where travel was constant, for any travel done on project funds. Since the state project leaders were in charge of the collection of data in the individual states and more or less distant from the Regional Office, this procedure became unworkable, particularly in view of the fact that the setup prescribed that the Chairman of the Regional Committee as well as the Project Director sign these requisitions.

Obviously many necessary trips would have been held up had the states waited in each instance for such authorization to clear officially through the University business office. A system of blanket requisitions was later developed which worked satisfactorily. Under this procedure a single requisition covered the expense for each man or group of men for a period of six months or a year so that a separate requisition for each trip was unnecessary. Theoretically, under the old system the Project Director and the committee chairman had to pass on the desirability of almost every move in the entire region before it was made. During the collection of the data with as many as twenty-five men moving almost continuously it can readily be seen that this was a full-time job and one which put an unnecessary burden particularly on the committee chairman who intended to devote only a small fraction of his time to project work. Under these circumstances it was of course impossible for him to keep up with the detail of the activities. Under the blanket requisition system, the Project Director was in constant touch with the work in all parts of the region but was not under the necessity of going through the form of appearing to pass on each individual travel plan. Moreover, as already indicated, the committee plan provided that this detailed supervision of the field work within the states be left to the state project leaders. Other illustrations of similar problems and adjustments might be given.

In addition to matters of adjustment occasioned by the difference in physical scope of the state and the region were the matters affected by the temporary nature of the Regional Project as compared with the permanent nature of the host University. The regulations on terminal leave may be used as an illustration. The host University had a regulation prohibiting terminal leave. That is to say, the payroll period could not terminate with leave status. Obviously such a regulation could not apply in the same way to a temporary project as to an institution which offers the possibility of permanent employment. In such matters as well as in a number of others it should be recognized at the outset that a given state university is geared to the needs of the particular state in which it functions and that adjustments must necessarily be made to conform to the needs of a regional undertaking.

In general the working arrangement between the Project and the university should be devised in such way so as to assure that the university acts only as a disbursing agency and that it in no way becomes involved in the policies of the Project. The university officials, having agreed to disperse the funds in accordance with the wishes of the Project, have no further decisions to make. Their cooperation henceforth is routine. This routine should be reduced to the minimum necessary to meet legal requirements so as not to burden the officials with unnecessary paper work and also to guard against any chance of red tape delay or interference with the working of the Project. To this end the Project should establish direct relations with the business office in handling the detail of the business matters and thus eliminate burdening the university officials with items which are not of immediate concern to them and for which, by the nature of the project agreement, they are not officially responsible.

THE PROBLEM OF SALARY LEVELS

It has already been indicated that a most important consideration in choosing a disbursing agency and headquarters for the project concerned the willingness of the university in question to cooperate with the Project. But before it is possible for any agency to say what it will or will not do it is necessary that the nature of the cooperation demanded be laid before it in detail. If the university in question cannot meet the demands which it is necessary for the project to place upon it, this fact should be known in advance so that other arrangements can be made.

One of the most serious difficulties encountered in the Regional Project concerned the matter of salary levels, particularly with reference to secretarial and clerical employees. At the time of the selection of the project headquarters the Regional Committee understood that the regional funds were to be disbursed as it indicated and without question. This was likewise the understanding of the Foundations which had granted the funds, since they were granted for use by the region as a whole and not for an individual state. Although generally understood by all concerned, the detailed implications of such an arrangement were not fully appreciated by the disbursing agency.

As a result the University refused to confirm certain appointments as recommended by the Project Director on the basis that the salary level was higher than that maintained by the University. The Project Director took the matter to the Regional Committee. The Committee took the view that it had complete control over indicating how the funds should be disbursed. The Project Director was therefore authorized to lay the whole matter before the University officials. The University officials however refused to accept the appointment in question as recommended by the Project because of the proximity of University departments with a lower salary schedule. This created a serious situation as to the immediate conduct of the Project and its basic relation to the University.

Several lines of action were considered. A first alternative was that the headquarters move to one of the other states. At this time the Project had been in operation approximately ten months and had assembled a regional staff, several of whom had moved long distances with their families. To have changed the headquarters would have involved considerable trouble and expense and it was thought wise to avoid such a move if at all possible. A second alternative was to get an off-campus location in the same city and arrange to have the funds handled through one of the local banks. Inquiries were made and such a move was regarded as feasible in case no better arrangement presented itself. However, in the course of these negotiations, the University administration indicated that the University would continue to handle the project funds and disburse them as indicated by the Project, provided the project headquarters were moved from the campus to the city. This appeared to be a satisfactory solution to the problem.

Accordingly suitable office space was found and the Project set up its headquarters several blocks from the campus. No further difficulty was encountered with respect to university acceptance of project recommendations. Otherwise project relations with the University remained exactly as they had been before. All appointments and all business of the Project continued to be handled through the University as formerly. Following the removal of the headquarters from the campus the project wage scale was revised slightly upward both in order to attract more efficient workers and also to prevent excessive turnover. Even so, the Project lost several key employees to the University largely because of the more permanent tenure which it offered as compared with the temporary tenure offered by the Project. The experience of the Project would indicate, in line with what might be generally expected, that a higher wage must be paid to secure services of equal quality in a temporary as compared with a permanent organization.

Apart from the point at issue both advantages and disadvantages resulted from physically separating the project headquarters from the campus. But all in all the advantages appear to have outweighed the disadvantages. Much of the IBM machine work was done on the campus but the distance was short and little inconvenience resulted. Possibly the greatest inconvenience had to do with the mail. All official project material dealing with the business office had either to be mailed or carried over, which occasionally caused slight delay. Campus notices addressed to the regional staff were also frequently delayed. Then also, there was the matter of responsibility of the Project for the building which it occupied, but here again the problem was very minor. There was, of course, the financial disadvantage of paying rent for facilities which had been furnished free on the campus. Relatively, however, this was a minor item on the budget.

These disadvantages were probably more than offset by the freedom and *esprit de corps* which the Project was able to achieve in its separate location. There was less feeling of attachment to a particular state and more to the region. Moreover, the off-campus setting provided an ideal place for the workers' conferences. The workers did not have the feeling that they were visiting the headquarters University but rather that they were coming together on a strictly regional basis. They regarded the Project headquarters with a sense of proprietorship which would have been difficult to achieve with the office space on the campus.[2]

The Project would however have missed several advantages had moving from the campus also meant a complete separation from the University. With the University connection the various facilities on the campus were open to the project employees. In addition, transportation and various other expenditures were allowed freedom from taxation which would not have been the case had the funds been handled by a private agency. It should be pointed out that the fine personal relations which existed between the regional staff members and their families and those of the University were in no way impaired by the movement of the Project from the campus.

In appraising in general the situation which arose regarding salary levels it may be observed that several factors operated to make this a more crucial problem in the experience of this project than might have been the case under other circumstances. In the first place, the salary levels for secretarial and clerical workers at the host University were lower than in any of the other cooperating schools. Secondly, the project was in operation during the war emergency at which time it was most difficult to avoid a considerable personnel turnover.

2. The Project headquarters was an old brick southern colonial home with large rooms and spacious yard. The huge dining room served as an excellent meeting room for the workers' conferences and incidentally as a frequent meeting place for social get-togethers and meals particularly at the time of these conferences. The *esprit de corps* of the group was doubtless greatly promoted by these congenial physical arrangements. It might be mentioned in this connection that as an outgrowth of the workers' conferences the Project workers published and circulated a News Letter during the life of the Project to the entire Project worker connection.

CHAPTER SEVEN

Concluding Statement

The real meaning of the Regional Project experience cannot be understood apart from a consideration of the conditions under which the Project operated. Hence, there is no attempt in this brief concluding statement to summarize the various points that have been made in the body of this report.

Fundamentally, the procedures of scientific research are the same in regional work as anywhere else. Their application, however, needs to be considered carefully in order to fit the particular needs of regional endeavor.

It has been pointed out that the following items, among others, gave particular concern in the conduct of the Regional Project: definition of research objectives; delegation of research responsibility; functions of sponsoring committee as related to those of the research workers; clearance of administrative matters with disbursing agency; administrative arrangements within the project organization; coordination of subject matter fields; status of regional workers while in the several states; workers' acceptance of subject matter aims of Committee; coordination of state data; and workers' conferences.

The above items are discussed in the body of the report. In addition, because of the urgent demand for guidance in the field of regional research, the writer feels impelled to set down several broad impressions growing out of the Regional Research Project experience.

In the first place, as to the advisability of regional research itself, there would appear to be no question. The question concerns the type of regional research to be undertaken.

Earlier in this report, two broad types of regional research collaboration are indicated, *coordinated* and *cooperative*. The Regional Project had as its goal cooperative rather than simply coordinated research. Its organization cannot be understood apart from that fact.

The methods of cooperative research include those of coordinated research. But they include even more. They include the mechanisms for the regional group to work, not only on allied and related subjects, but to work *together* through the research processes on a common body of data. In the Regional Project this meant the use of a uniform field schedule in the several states. Thoroughgoing cooperative research demands joint action through all the research procedures beginning with the selection of the problem and following through the formulation of hypotheses, observation, classification of materials, and the construction of the final report. Obviously this "joint action" may be broken off at any given stage of the research procedure with a substitution therefore of a looser form of collaboration. In this way the two research approaches are fused, as indeed they are certain to be in most undertakings. Although the emphasis in the present study was on cooperative research, a number of the state bulletins published in connection with the project were based only partially on the project data. Thus they were the result of both coordinated and cooperative effort as the terms are herein defined.

Obviously a pure type of cooperative research collaboration is not always feasible. A loose collaboration might serve the purpose better. On the other hand, if cooperative collaboration is possible, it will yield rather far-reaching results.

Since the present project has been of the cooperative type, some of the important advantages which have come to light in this experience may be noted:

(1) It has made possible the fusion on a common problem of several subject matter fields. This would have been impossible had the workers had less close contact with each other. This fusion of disciplines is fundamental in that an adequate understanding of the subject at hand could not have been made from a single type of approach.

(2) Close integration among the state workers resulted in common and improved definitions making possible (a) exact comparisons between the several states (b) a regional product

of a nature otherwise unattainable (c) a larger body of data from which to draw generalizations.

(3) Close collaboration among the workers in the region on common data gave greater inter-stimulation and mutual aid than could have been possible had each been working on a separate phase of the subject, even though in general collaboration with the others. This point was amply demonstrated in the effectiveness of the workers' conferences where not only were ideas exchanged but new and detailed techniques of research resulted from the meeting of minds on the specific research data. The heads of departments testify to an intellectual growth of their departmental members through association with the regional work. Mentioned particularly were factors of intellectual stimulation and practical aid in research techniques. For effectual cooperation there must be a common meeting ground. In research this can be most effectually attained by centering on a common problem with an integrated body of research data.

By and large it may be assumed that all regional research has a strong element of commonality and that the problems encountered as between different regional endeavours vary more in intensity and detail than in major content. In this as in other similar matters the suggestion is frequently made that the only way the individual can learn is by going through the experience himself. True, the cooperators in this project definitely feel that they are not starting from "scratch" in getting a new regional program under way. But they are also definitely convinced that a major part of what they have learned may be transmitted to others of similar interests if they care to study with reasonable diligence the experiences of this project. The following broad suggestions for regional research cooperation are indicated in the hope that they may be of value to those whose interest it is to undertake research of this nature.

1. Regional Research Organization

In the first place, there should be in the region an over-all sponsoring committee or council. In college- and university-sponsored research, this would logically comprise heads of the departments or others of similar status and function from the various fields of interest to be represented in the studies contemplated. In addition, it should have at least one member who is a dean or director of one of the cooperating Experiment Stations who can then act as a liaison representative between the Committee and the other agricultural college officials of the region. Should other organizations be represented in the research, they should also have appropriate liaison personnel on this committee.

The function of this group should be that of sponsorship and administration. Its title should be such as to suggest only the broad area in which it intends to operate, without reference to specific disciplines or problems. Such a title as The Regional Social Science Committee (with appropriate regional designation) would sufficiently indicate the broad area of operation.

It should be emphasized that this is not a working committee in the sense of carrying forward research detail. Its function should be (1) to assess the research needs of the region, (2) to select and make available the necessary sub-committee personnel, (3) to decide upon the broad area of research to be undertaken and, in conjunction with those selected to do the research, upon the specific objectives of the project contemplated, (4) as persons in positions of administrative responsibility, to facilitate the activity of those on the sub-committees engaged in the actual subject matter research, (5) to enlist the support of the administrative officials of their respective institutions by conferring with them at all stages of Regional Project development and progress, (6) to receive the reports from the sub-committees responsible for carrying forward the work.

At such time as the over-all committee, described above, decides upon a problem of regional interest and scope, it appoints an appropriate sub-committee. This is the working committee, corresponding in the present project to the Workers' Conference, a descriptive title for which would have been the Land Tenure Sub-Committee. This sub-committee constitutes the central focus of the research effort. Upon it rests the responsibility for the research work. Within the limits of its assignment it should not only be given freedom to proceed, but its activities should be facilitated in every way possible by the over-all committee. In this way the sub-committee becomes a responsible professional group and the authority on the subject it undertakes.

The relation of the sub-committee to the over-all committee should be much the same as that of the department member to the head of his department. Actually, that is the relationship under the suggested arrangement since for the most part these sub-committee members are responsible in their respective departments to individual members of the over-all committee. It should be pointed out that the committee arrangement suggested above does not prevent an over-all committee member from serving on the technical, subject matter sub-committee should he desire to do active work on the particular project undertaken. In fact, this would constitute a highly desirable arrangement.

It is entirely possible that several sub-committees may be operating simultaneously under the over-all committee. In this case, the sub-committee would normally, of course, be composed of different personnel. It is deemed essential, however, that the work of a given sub-committee be sufficiently broad to encompass the several subject matter aspects of the project in question. This usually means that several subject matter disciplines are included since in few instances does any single one of them cover sufficient scope to answer questions of general significance. This project would have lost one of its strongest assets had the workers' conferences been divided into separate units of land economics, farm management, and rural sociology. It is entirely possible that some highly specialized problems demand only one subject matter field for their solution, but this would seem to be the exception rather than the rule. Although the reason is not clear, the experience of the present project indicates that research cooperation among the several disciplines proceeded much better on the regional than on the individual state level.

2. THE WORK GROUP

The key group in regional research is obviously the workers' group, called the Workers' Conference group in the present project. This group may be referred to by other names such as a sub-committee, working committee, technical committee, etc. It is the group, however, which forms the hypotheses and does the technical research. All phases of the organization should point toward facilitating the work of this group.

3. CENTRAL OFFICE AND DIRECTOR

A central coordinating head is necessary. The size of the staff depends on the division of the detailed work between the states and such central staff. Also, the work involved will vary greatly with the nature of the project and the type of regional collaboration. *Cooperative* research collaboration will require a stronger central nucleus than *coordinated* research. The physical headquarters should be established in one of the collaborating states.

The function of the director or coordinator should be that of coordinating the subject matter work of the project. He should be furnished with suitable administrative aid so that his time is not distracted unduly from the subject matter pursuits of the work. He should act as a liaison between the over-all committee and the working group but should be an active member of the working group. He should have a hand in the planning of the work that is to be undertaken.

4. REGIONAL RESEARCH TECHNIQUES

Regional research techniques are essentially no different from those employed in non-regional research. The research principles are the same. But as in any large scale undertaking, the problems of coordination demand relatively greater effort. The efficiency with which the detail of the coordination is handled in large measure determines the effectiveness of the regional approach. The will to cooperate must be strongly fortified by mechanisms to facilitate the cooperation.

5. COLLABORATION OF SUBJECT MATTER FIELDS

Though not absolutely essential, it is highly desirable that several subject matter fields collaborate. Few practical questions can be answered by a single discipline. Furthermore, inter-discipline collaboration is greatly facilitated by regional endeavour.

6. DEFINITION OF THE REGION

The area covered by a regional study need not be homogeneous in all major aspects. But it must necessarily have an element of commonality concerning the items under consideration. Regions may be constituted differently according to the nature of the subject matter being considered.

7. VALUES OF REGIONAL RESEARCH

Among others, the following chief advantages of regional cooperation were noted in the present project: (1) Close integration between the work in the several states made for unified definitions and working concepts. This resulted in making possible detailed comparison of data, a regional product, and a broader base for scientific generalization. (2) Because of the wide scope and varied personnel, the regional cooperative approach made possible a more effective fusion of the subject matter specialties on a common problem than would otherwise have been possible. (3) Greater professional stimulation and growth among the research workers of the region. (4) Elimination of duplicate work between states.

8. Efficiency in Use of Funds

The question is frequently raised as to whether, from a research standpoint, the money expended on a regional project would be more advantageously utilized if it were divided among the cooperating states and spent individually by them without regard to regional collaboration.

This question is largely irrelevant in that the emphasis of the two procedures is different. In the present project great emphasis was placed on developing better research procedures through mutual aid among the states, a goal which is largely out of the reach of individual state research. The results of this experience were encouraging and satisfactory. Again, wider coverage and combination of state data allowed for more accurate generalization than could have been possible on an individual state basis. In the present study many false conclusions were forestalled by comparisons of identical data between the states. Generalizations, though harder to reach, are eminently sounder and of wider application when reached from the vantage of a wide regional base. A further aspect of regional inter-state cooperation, not a part of individual state research, constitutes the stimulation and development of state personnel through the wider contacts. After observing the effect of the workers' conferences on their departmental personnel, several of the committee members have rated this as one of the most important values of regional cooperation.

9. Major Difficulties and Remedies

(1) Selection of a research subject. With a number of people involved, it is difficult to select a research subject which will focus interest and effectively maintain the cooperation of the group over the necessary period of time. In order to enlist the interest of as many people as possible, the Regional Project first stated its objectives broadly. The scope proved too broad to be manageable, and as the focus was narrowed, some of the cooperators lost interest. A great deal of energy needs to be expended in the initial stages in meticulously defining the research objectives. The

broad field of the research endeavor should be selected by the over-all committee, but the special research objectives should be worked out by those whose duty it is to carry forward the research. Only in this way are they likely to have the necessary interest and enthusiasm to carry the project through to successful conclusion.

(2) Individual research methods. Changing the deep-seated pattern of individual research procedure constitutes a major problem. Research cooperation includes all of the problems of cooperation in general. But in addition, cooperation in research requires realignment of much past research experience from an individualistic to a group point of view. This transition is rendered more difficult since it involves a rearrangement of individual incentives for achievement and new methods of determining individual credit for group products. The stimulation of group work, however, once it is experienced goes far to offset these difficulties. Moreover, the output of the individual state worker is enhanced and he has a chance to be a part of a much larger and more significant undertaking than would otherwise be possible. However serious these difficulties may be, as with the biological, physical and other sciences, the current problems of the social sciences require such elaborate techniques that they cannot be satisfied apart from multiple effort.

(3) Identification with the region. Conventionally the tasks of the state research worker have been in terms of one state only. The problem is to extend this identification to encompass the region. Although this was partially achieved in the present project, the record is marked by a too general attitude of detachment toward the region by most of the state workers and department heads. At the beginning of this project there was little incentive from the Agricultural Experiment Stations for state workers to undertake regional work. On the contrary, the state worker's success was gauged mainly by his contributions to the state in question. Although this general situation may be expected to continue, the introduction of federal funds earmarked for regional use is giving a new and substantial incentive to regional work and thinking.

Identification with the region may best be achieved by educating all concerned personnel as to the advantages of regional endeavor, particularly as they concern the contemplated research.

The enthusiasms of the over-all committee need to be shared by the worker groups. Those who are to carry forward the detailed project research need to be in on the ground floor of the planning. Too often, particularly where travel is involved, it is the members of the over-all committee who attend the meetings. Plans are developed and enthusiasms are engendered which may or may not be shared by those upon whose shoulders the success or failure of the undertaking will finally fall. These latter individuals need to be a part of the project planning from its early stages.

Once an area of research has been decided upon by the over-all committee, the responsible research workers should henceforth be in attendance at all meetings which purport to deal with the subject matter of the project. In this way they will tend to identify themselves not only with the subject matter of the project but with the whole undertaking as a regional endeavor. Finally, it should be pointed out that the most effective regional identification will be achieved through joint work on concrete research materials rather than through meetings which praise regional cooperation but which yield no tangible issue of research results.

(4) Turnover of personnel. To the extent that regional work is done on a temporary project basis, the problems of securing suitable personnel are multiplied. As regional efforts come to be manned more largely by regular state employees and others as a part of their regular tasks, this difficulty can be partially overcome. Meanwhile, the cooperating agencies can greatly aid by granting leaves of absence where the nature of the work does not allow direct transfer of the personnel to the regional task. Turnover of cooperating state personnel was one of the greatest practical hindrances to the present project. The problem in this instance was greatly magnified because of war conditions. Normally this should not constitute a serious difficulty.

10. REGIONAL USE OF TERMS AND CONCEPTS

Differences in the interpretation of research terms and concepts was surprisingly evident in the workers' conferences. As a result a regional glossary of terms was developed. Had the individuals worked separately, many of these discrepancies would never have been uncovered and spurious inter-state comparisons based on inaccurate terminology would have persisted.

11. WRITING THE REPORTS

The Regional Project developed two types of reports, state and regional. The actual writing of the state reports should be done by the state personnel utilizing regional materials in so far as possible. Regional reports should be written by those who are in a position to devote their attention to the region as a whole for the specific subject under consideration. As indicated elsewhere in this report, this work might best be done through technical sub-committees. In preparation for the reports, the plan of tabulation should be developed by the working group as a whole, with such specialized subject matter sub-groups as may facilitate the task. However, because of the necessity of working out cross tabulations and other points of cooperation and uniformity among the sub-interests of the larger group, the larger group should be continuously advised as to the work of the smaller groups.

12. FUNCTIONS OF INDIVIDUALS AND GROUPS

Effective cooperation demands the clear definition of individual and group roles. For all major items, decisions will normally be made by the group in question. Failure to define functions, duties, and makes for general inefficiency. Application of this principle and responsibilities of individuals and groups leads to friction may easily be overlooked in regional research because of the scope and detail of the arrangements. Furthermore there is the frequent temptation to keep matters indefinite under the illusion that harmony may be achieved in this way. Of principal concern in this connection is the function of the regional or sponsoring committee as related to the workers' groups, the relation of the project director or coordinator to the committee and the workers groups, the relations of state and regional employees, and the relation of the research group as a whole to its disbursing agency. Needless to say, once they are made, decisions need to be adhered to by all concerned.

13. IMPLICATIONS OF COOPERATIVE ACTIVITY

All cooperating personnel should understand as fully as possible the implications of working together before the actual work begins. It should be pointed out to them that although there is ample place for individual performance, in items of major concern all members must acquiesce to the decisions of the group. The advantages as well as the disadvantages should be considered.

The experience of the present project indicates that talking about cooperation without tangible materials at hand produces less results and is more likely to result in friction than where there are definite and tangible research materials upon which to work. This conclusion is drawn from the experience of the workers' conferences which were addressed to concrete research materials as contrasted with certain other meetings held in connection with the project in which the burden of consideration concerned talking about cooperation and arranging for it rather than actually carrying on the work. Although carrying forward the actual research may yield the greatest satisfaction, it should be emphasized that setting up the working organization is most necessary and important.

14. FUNDS FOR REGIONAL RESEARCH

Although the present project operated to a considerable extent on funds provided by private agencies it is believed that aid from sources other than those provided by the governmental agencies is not necessary, provided an effective coordinating arrangement can be set up within the region. In this project, much of the work, other than coordination, done by the regional staff could have been done by those employed by the states. Under this plan, however, it would have been necessary for the states to have invested more heavily in personnel than was the case. In this project, for example, the regional staff paid by outside funds wrote the regional report. The state personnel wrote the state reports. A merger of these two tasks would have been possible and desirable had the cooperating states been able to invest the necessary personnel.

It should be made clear that regional collaboration can be carried on and in fact is now being done in several regions with a minimum of outside aid. Moreover, an increasing amount of Agricultural Experiment Station funds are being set aside for regional research. As those in charge of public funds become increasingly convinced that expenditures for regional research actually economize the use of funds by the prevention of overlapping work and at the same time yield exceedingly valuable results, not attainable in smaller areas, the problem of source of funds will loom less large than at present. In fact, probably the chief concern of research workers even at this time should not be the source of funds with

which to carry on regional research but rather the presentation of
well-laid plans for the utilization of regional funds as they
become available.

APPENDIX

SAMPLE OF SUMMARY OF CODE. Copies of these were sent to each of the tenure workers in the region for the seventeen statistical cards as they were developed. The *Summary of Code* as contrasted with the *Code* constitutes a compact indication of the coverage of the card. The *italicized* words are key items which are defined in the *Explanation of Codes*. In this, as well as in the examples of other similar items included in the Appendix, the chief purpose of the illustrations is to show some of the methods by which the collaboration was carried forward. Detailed mechanisms of this kind are of prime importance in cooperative research and need to be meticulously worked out.

CARD 7 — LEASING ARRANGEMENTS
SUMMARY OF CODE
Farm and Family Schedule
Regional Land Tenure Research Project

Column Number	Items[1]	Location on Schedule		
		Sec.	line	column
1	Number of *card*			
2	Name of *state*	A		
3	*Color* and national origin	A		
4	Present *tenure status* of head	A		
5	Cropland, *acres* in	D		
6	Value of *farm business*	E, L		
7	Gross *income*	B[2]		P
8	*Soil* classification	A, D		
9	*Type of farming*	D, L, M		
10	*Socio-economic status* scale	B[3]		
11	Migration index (*moves*)	K		
12	Parents, *tenure status* of	B	1, 2	J
13	Years of earning life (*tenure change*)	K	2	
14	Stage in *family cycle*	B		
15	Degree of *management* index	F, H		
16	Farm *income*, percent of gross income	B[4]		
17	Cotton, five-year average *yield* of	D		
18	Net worth (*farm business*)	E, J, L		
19	Productive livestock, *animal units* of	L		
20	Type of power and size of *equipment*	E-2		
21	Diversification index (*type of farming*)	D, L		
22	Type of *lease*—form and length	H	1, 2	
23	Property covered by *lease*	D, E, H, L		
24	Crop method of *rental payment*	H	6	
25	Livestock method of *rental payment*	H	5, 6	
26	Ratio of *rental payment* to farm business rented	D[5]		
27	Wages from landlord, percent of gross *income*	B[2]		
28	Color and sex of *landlord*	F	4a, b	
29	Occupation of *landlord*	F	4a	
30	Kinship to *landlord*	K	3	A
31	Distance from farm to residence of *landlord*	F	2b	
32	Frequency of supervision by *landlord*	H	11a, b	
33	Rent tract index of *management*	F, H		
34	Families supervised by *landlord*, number of	A, F-5		
35	Source of production and furnish *credit*	J, H-11		
36	Housing, *socio-economic status*	C		
37	Crop *yield* index	D		

1. **Words** italicized are key words to alphabetical list of Explanation of Codes
2. Also Sections D; L; M; and P, column (C)
3. Also Sections C; E-2; and Q-1
4. Also Sections D; L; M; and P-1
5. Also Sections E; H-6; L; and M

Appendix 1

CARD 7 — LEASING ARRANGEMENTS
Summary of Code (Cont'd)

Column Number	Items[1]	Location on Schedule		
		Sec.	line	column
38	Head or spouse, highest *education* of	B	1, 2	I
39	Rent tract, years on (*moves*)	K		
40	Age of *landlord*	F	4c	
41	Inventory of buildings and poultry, *division* of	H-5a	2, 3, 8	
42	Inventory of cattle and hogs, *division* of	H-5a	4, 6	
43	Inventory of machinery and power, *division* of	H-5a	7, 8	
44	Cottonseed expenses, *division* of	H-5c	2 3	
45	Cotton fertilizer expense, *division* of	H-5c	5	
46	Harvesting expense, *division* of	H-7		A, B
47	Ginning expense, *division* of	H-5c		
48	Spray material expense, *division* of	H-5c	6	
49	Hauling expense for cash crops, *division* of	H-7		E, F
50	Processing expense (other than ginning), *division* of	H-7		C, D
51	Machine hire expense, *division* of	H-5c		
52	Repair cost for materials for dwelling, *division* of	E-1, H-5	6	
53	Repair costs for materials for "other" *division* of	E-1, H-5	7	
54	Hauling expense for cotton, *division* of	H-7	1	E, F
55	Unpaid labor on improvement repair, *division* of	E-1	15	
56	Cotton lint production, *division* of	D, H-5b	-, 1	
57	Cottonseed production, *division* of	D, H-5b	-, 2	
58	Feed crop production, *division* of	D, H-5b		
59	Other cash crop production, *division* of	D, H-5b		
60	Peanut production, *division* of	D, H-5b		
61	Alfalfa seed production, *division* of	D, H-5b		
62	Alfalfa hay production, *division* of	D, H-5b		
63	AAA payments, *division* of	H-5b	3, 4, 5	
64	Arrangements for present *lease*	K	15	
65-66	Frequency of supervision—visits from *landlord*	H	11a	
67-68	Frequency of supervision—visits to *landlord*	H	11b	
69	Selection of crops and acres, division of *management*	H-11c	1, 2	
70	Selection of kind and amount of livestock, division of *management*	H-11c	3, 4	
71	Planting and cultivating, division of *management*	H-11d	1, 2	
72	Harvesting and securing fertilizer, division of *management*	H-11d	3, 4	
73	Production and furnish credit, division of *management*	H-11d	5, 6	
74	Crop rotation and marketing, division *management*	H-11d	7, 8	
75	Record keeping and AAA responsibility, division of *management*	H-11d	9, 10	
76	Delivery of feed crop rent (*division*)	H-7		E, F
77	Number of *lease*	H		
78-79-80	Number of *schedule*	A		

6. Section E-1, line 2, cols. D and E; and H-5c, line 15, cols. A and B
7. Section E-1, lines 3 to 12, cols. D and E; and section H-5c, lines 17 and 18, cols. A and B

SAMPLE OF CODE. Copies of these were sent to each of the tenure workers in the region for each of the seventeen statistical cards as they were developed. These indicate the detail of the code. The *italicized* words are key items which are defined in the *Explanation of Codes*. It will be noted that the coding is not always identical for all states but that it is set up in so far as possible so that all items are comparable. In order to save space the accompanying sample includes only the first forty of the eighty columns of Card 7.

CARD 7—LEASING ARRANGEMENTS

Code

Farm and Family Schedule
Regional Land Tenure Research Project

Column Number	Code and Item			Location on Schedule
1	7	Number of *card*		
2		Name of *state*		Section A
	1	Arkansas		
	2	Louisiana		
	3	Mississippi		
	4	Oklahoma		
	5	Texas		
	6	Special FSA Study (Arkansas)		
3		*Color* and national origin		Section A
		Oklahoma	Texas	Other States
	1	Native white	Native white	White
	2	Other (German, Russian, Negro, Mexican)	Negro and Mexican	Negro
	3	. . . .	Czech	. . . .
	4	. . . .	German	. . . .
4		Present *tenure status* of head		Section A
	1	Full owner		
	2	Part owner		
	3	Indeterminate tenure[1]		
	4	Cash or standing renter		
	5	Share renter		
	6	Share-cash renter		
	7	Cropper		
	8	Tenant other than specified		
	9	Laborer		
	0	Other (non-farm, non-operating owner)		

1. Derived from multiple sources. Some items were edited as a summary number in green on the printed schedules. Others were computed on work sheets.

Column Number	Code and Item			Location on Schedule
5	Cropland, *acres* in			Section D

		Oklahoma	Texas	Other States
	0	0.0	0.0	0.0
	1	0.1-	0.1-	0.1-
	2	20.0-	20.0-	10.0-
	3	40.0-	40.0-	20.0-
	4	80.0-	60.0-	30.0-
	5	120.0-	80.0-	40.0-
	6	140.0-	100.0-	50.0-
	7	160.0-	120.0-	60.0-
	8	240.0-	160.0-	80.0-
	9	320.0-	200.0-	100.0-
	X	640.0-	280.0-	160.0-
	Y	N.A.	N.A.	N.A.

Column Number	Code and Item			Location on Schedule
6	Value of *farm business*			*Sections E and L

		Oklahoma	Texas	Other States
	0	$ 0.00	$ 0.00	$ 0.00
	1	0.01-	0.01-	0.01
	2	1,500.00-	1,500.00-	500.00-
	3	3,500.00-	3,500.00-	1,000.00-
	4	5,500.00-	5,500.00-	1,500.00-
	5	7,500.00-	7,500.00-	2,000.00-
	6	11,500.00-	9,500.00-	2,500.00-
	7	15,500.00-	11,500.00-	3,500.00-
	8	23,500.00-	15,500.00-	5,500.00-
	9	31,500.00-	23,500.00-	7,500.00-
	X	63,500.00-	31,500.00-	15,500.00-
	Y	N.A.	N.A.	N.A.

Column Number	Code and Item			Location on Schedule
7	Gross *income*			*Sections B, col. (P); D; L; M; and P. col. (C)

		Oklahoma	Texas	Other States
	0	$ 0.00	$ 0.00	$ 0.00
	1	400.00-	200.00-	200.00-
	2	800.00-	400.00-	400.00-
	3	1,600.00-	800.00-	600.00-
	4	2,400.00-	1,200.00-	800.00-
	5	3,200.00-	1,600.00-	1,200.00-
	6	4,800.00-	2,000.00-	1,600.00-
	7	6,400.00-	2,400.00-	2,400.00-
	8	9,600.00-	3,200.00-	3,200.00-
	9	12,800.00-	6,400.00-	6,400.00-
	Y	N.A.	N.A.	N.A.

Column Number	Code and Item				Location on Schedule
8		*Soil* classification			Sections A and D

		Arkansas[1]	Mississippi[2]	Oklahoma[3]	Other States[4]
1		Orangeburg	111	Medium	Under 100
2		Luverne	121	Coarse	100-
3		Ruston	211	Fine	125-
4		Thomasville	221	Mixed	150-
5		Norfolk	112	....	175-
6		Kirvin	321	....	200-
7		Susquehanna	231, 113	....	225-
8		Caddo	122, 222	....	250-
9		Terrace soils (Cahaba, Kalmia, Myatt)	123, 331	....	....
Y		....		N.A.	N.A.
R		Houston, ... Bibb, Norfolk sand, Ocklockonee, Caddo silt loam, Susquehanna silt loam, and Susquehanna silty clay loam	....	....

1. Overpunches are used as follows: Y—fine sandy loam; X—very fine sandy loam and gravelly very fine sandy loam; O—sandy loam; and R—all others. Ruston sand and Ruston fine sandy loam, smooth phase, are included with fine sandy loam. A code of R is handled as a blank on the card.

2. Overpunches are used as follows: Y—good soils; X—medium soils; and O—poor soils. The numbers used in the code represent the score given to the cropland by the enumerator for degree of slope, degree of erosion and seriousness of the drainage problem reading from left to right. A score of "111" denotes level land, with little or no erosion, and no drainage problem.

3. Refers to texture of soil.

4. Five-year average cotton yield.

Column Number	Code and Item			Location on Schedule
9		*Type of farming*		*Sections D; L; and M

		Oklahoma	Texas	Other States
1		Crop farms	Cotton	Cotton
2		Cotton-general	Cotton-livestock	Cotton-livestock
3		Cotton-wheat-general	Livestock-cotton	Cotton-truck
4		Livestock-general	....	General
5		....	....	Incidental or subsistence
6		None	None	None
Y		N.A.	N.A.	N.A.

Column Number	Code and Item		Location on Schedule
10		*Socio-economic status* scale	*Sections B; C; E-2; and Q-1
	0	104 - 113	
	1	114 - 125	
	2	124 - 133	
	3	134 - 143	
	4	144 - 153	
	5	154 - 163	
	6	164 - 173	
	7	174 - 183	
	8	184 - 193	
	9	194 - 203	
	X	204 - 213	
11		Migration index *(moves)*	*Section K
	X	0.1	
	0	0.2	
	1	0.3	
	2	0.4	
	3	0.5 - 0.6	
	4	0.7 - 0.9	
	5	1.0 - 1.4	
	6	1.5 - 2.1	
	7	2.2 - 3.1	
	8	3.2 - 4.6	
	9	4.7 - 6.8	
	Y	N.A.	
12		Parents, *tenure status* of	Section B, col. (J),
	1	Both sets of parents owners	lines 1 and 2
	2	One set owners, other set renters	
	3	One set owners, other set croppers	
	4	Both sets renters	
	5	Both sets croppers, or one set renters and other set croppers	
	6	One set renters, other set croppers	
	7	One set croppers, other set laborers	
	8	One set owners, other set laborers	
	9	Both sets laborers	
	Y	Both sets N.A., both sets non-farm or combination of N.A. and non-farm	

(If farm tenure of only one set of parents is given, code as if both sets had that tenure)

Column Number	Code and Item	Location on Schedule
13	Years of earning life *(tenure change)*	Section K, line 2

1	0 - 4
2	5 - 9
3	10 - 19
4	20 - 29
5	30 - 39
6	40 - 49
7	50 - 59
8	60 and over
Y	N.A.

| 14 | Stage in *family* cycle | Section B |

1	Married, childless couple, wife less than 45 years of age
2	Married, family with oldest child less than 14 years of age
3	Married, family with oldest child between 14 and 35 years of age
4	Married, childless couple with wife 45 years of age or over
5	Married, family with oldest child 36 years of age or over
6	Broken family, childless, wife less than 45 years of age
7	Broken family, with oldest child less than 14 years of age
8	Broken family, with oldest child between 14 and 35 years of age
9	Broken family, childless, wife over 45 years of age
0	Broken family, with oldest child 36 years of age or over
Y	Single

(Broken is widowed or divorced, and possibly remarried)

| 15 | Degree of *management* index | *Section F, line 2b; and H |

	Oklahoma and Texas	Other States
1	0-	0-
2	10-	10-
3	20-	20-
4	40-	30-
5	60-	40-
6	70-	50-
7	75-	60-
8	80-	70-
9	85-	80-
X	90-	90-
Y	N.A.	N.A.

| 16 | Farm *income*, percent of gross income | *Sections B; D; L; M; and P-1 |

1	0.0 - 19.9
2	20.0 - 39.9
3	40.0 - 59.9
4	60.0 - 69.9
5	70.0 - 79.9
6	80.0 - 89.9
7	90.0 -100.0
Y	N.A.

Appendix 2

Column Number	Code and Item				Location on Schedule

17 — Cotton, five-year average *yield* of — Section D

	Mississippi	Oklahoma	Texas	Other States
0	1-	1-	1-	1-
1	50-	50-	50-	50-
2	100-	100-	100-	100-
3	150-	125-	125-	125-
4	200-	150-	150-	150-
5	250-	175-	175-	175-
6	300-	200-	200-	200-
7	350-	250-	225-	225-
8	400-	300-	250-	250-
9	450-	400-	. . .	300-
X	. . .	. . .	. . .	400
Y	N.A.	N.A.	N.A.	N.A.

18 — Net worth *(farm business)* — *Sections E, J, and L

0	Minus $500.00 or less
1	Minus $499.99 to minus $100.00
2	Minus $99.99 to plus $99.99
3	Plus $100.00 to plus $499.99
4	$500.00 to $1,299.99
5	$1,300.00 to $2,899.99
6	$2,900.00 to $6,099.99
7	$6,100.00 to $12,499.99
8	$12,500.00 to $25,299.99
9	$25,300.00 to $50,899.99
X	$50,900.00 to $102,099.99
Y	N.A.

19 — Productive livestock, *animal units* of — *Section L

	Oklahoma	Texas	Other States
0	0.00	0.00	0.00
1	0.01-	0.01-	0.01-
2	3.00-	1.00-	1.00-
3	5.00-	3.00-	2.00-
4	7.00-	5.00-	3.00-
5	9.00-	7.00-	4.00-
6	11.00-	9.00-	5.00-
7	15.00-	11.00-	7.00-
8	31.00-	15.00-	11.00-
9	63.00-	31.00-	15.00-
X	. . . .	. . . .	31.00-
Y	N.A.	N.A.	N.A.

Column Number	Code and Item		Location on Schedule

20		Type of power and size of *equipment*	Section E-2
	0	No power or equipment	
	1	1/2 row horse drawn equipment	
	2	1 row horse drawn equipment	
	3	2 row horse drawn equipment	
	4	1 row tractor equipment	
	5	2 row planter and cultivator, 1 bottom plow tractor equipment	
	6	2 row planter and cultivator, 2 bottom plow tractor equipment	
	7	1 row horse equipment and 1 row tractor equipment	
	8	1 row horse equipment and 2 row tractor equipment	
	9	2 row horse equipment and 2 two row tractor equipment	
	X	Half 1/2 row horse and half 1 row horse equipment	
	Y	N.A.	

21		Diversification index *(type of farming)*	*Sections D and L
	0	1.00 - 1.99	
	1	2.00 - 2.49	
	2	2.50 - 2.99	
	3	3.00 - 3.49	
	4	3.50 - 3.99	
	5	4.00 - 4.49	
	6	4.50 - 4.99	
	7	5.00 - 5.99	
	8	6.00 - 6.99	
	9	7.00 - 7.99	
	Y	N.A.	

22		Type of *lease*—form and length	Section H, Items 1,2
	1	Oral, automatic renewal	
	2	Oral, indefinite	
	3	Oral, one year, must be renewed	
	4	Written, one year	
	5	Written, three years	
	6	Written, five years	
	7	Written, 10 years	
	8	Written, 15 years	
	9	Written, 99 years	
	0	Written, other lengths	
	Y	N.A.	

Column Number	Code and Item	Location on Schedule
23	Property covered by *lease*	Sections D, E, H-6, and L

1	Farm unit
2	Pasture land only
3	Field rent only
4	Cropland only
5	Cropland and farmstead
6	Farmstead only
7	Equipment and workstock only
8	Cropland, farmstead, equipment and workstock
9	Farm unit and livestock lease
0	Other than specified
Y	N.A.

Column Number	Code and Item	Location on Schedule
24	Crop method of *rental payment*	Section H, Item 6

X	No cropland leased
0	No rent
1	Cash rent
2	Standing rent
3	1/4 and/or 1/3 share rent
4	1/2- share rent
5	1/4-1/3 share rent plus cash rent per acre
6	1/4-1/3 share rent plus bonus cash rent
7	Taxes, AAA check or "keep" of owner
8	Labor of "upkeep of place"
9	Other and combinations not specified
Y	N.A.

Column Number	Code and Item	Location on Schedule
25	Livestock method of *rental payment*	Section H, Items 5, 6

0	No livestock involved
1	Milk cow—calf rent
2	Poultry—one-half of poultry raised and products sold
3	Poultry—all of poultry raised and one-half of products sold
4	Milk cow (calf) and poultry (one-half of poultry raised and products sold)
5	Milk cow (calf) and poultry (all raised and one-half of products sold)
6	Complete livestock share lease
7	Joint family arrangement
9	Other arrangement

Column Number	Code and Item		Location on Schedule

26		Ratio of *rental payment* to farm business rented	Section D, E, H-6, L, M
	1	.55 and under	
	2	.56 - .99	
	3	1.0 - 1.7	
	4	1.8 - 3.1	
	5	3.2 - 5.5	
	6	5.6 - 9.9	
	7	10.0 - 17.7	
	8	17.8 - 31.5	
	9	31.6 - 56.1	
	0	56.2 - 99.9	
	X	100.0 and over	
	Y	N.A.	

27		Wages from landlord, per cent of gross *income*	Sections, D, L, M, and P-1
	0	None	
	1	0.1 - 9.9	
	2	10.0 - 19.9	
	3	20.0 - 29.9	
	4	30.0 - 39.9	
	5	40.0 - 49.9	
	6	50.0 - 59.9	
	7	60.0 - 69.9	
	8	70.0 - 79.9	
	9	80.0 - 89.9	
	X	90.0 - 100.0	
	Y	N.A.	

28		Color and sex of *landlord*	Section F, Items 4a, b
	1	White male	
	2	White female	Texas Special
	3	Negro male	
	4	Negro female	1 American male
	5	Other male	2 American female
	6	Other female	3 Czech male
	7	Estate, family administered	4 Czech female
	8	Estate, agent administered	5 German male
	9	Institution	6 German female
	0	Other	
	X	Individual with agent (overpunch)	
	Y	N.A.	

Column Number	Code and Item		Location on Schedule
29		Occupation of *landlord*	Section F, Item 4e
	1	Farm operator	
	2	Landlord or retired farmer	
	3	Farm agent	
	4	Professional occupation	
	5	Other occupation	
	6	Estate	
	7	Institution	
	Y	N.A.	
30		Kinship to *landlord*	Section K, line 3, column (A)
	0	None	
	1	Son or daughter	
	2	Son-in-law	
	3	Grandson	
	4	Grandson-in-law	
	5	Brother or sister	
	6	Brother-in-law or sister-in-law	
	7	Nephew, niece	
	8	Cousin	
	9	Other relationship	
	X	Not applicable (estate or institution)	
	Y	N.A.	
31		Distance from farm to residence of *landlord*	Section F, Item 2b
	0	Same house	
	1	.1 mile to .4 mile	
	2	.5-	
	3	1.0-	
	4	2.0-	
	5	5.0-	
	6	10.0-	
	7	25.0-	
	8	50.0-	
	9	100.0-	
	Y	N.A. and estate	
32		Frequency of supervision by *landlord*	Section H, Item 11a, b
	0	None and 1	
	1	2-4	
	2	5-9	
	3	10-24	
	4	25-49	
	5	50-99	
	6	100 and over	
	7	Daily	
	Y	N.A.	

Column Number	Code and Item			Location on Schedule
33		Rent tract index of *management*		Sections F, line 2;
		Oklahoma and Texas	Other States	H, Item 11
	1	0-	0-	
	2	10-	10-	
	3	20-	20-	
	4	40-	30-	
	5	60-	40-	
	6	70-	50-	
	7	75-	60-	
	8	80-	70-	
	9	85-	80-	
	X	90-	90-	
	Y	N.A.	N.A.	

34		Number of families supervised by *landlord* (actual number to 9)	Section A; F, line 5
	X	10 and over	
	Y	N.A.	

35		Source of production and furnish *credit*	Section J; H, Item 11
	0	No credit used	
	1	Landlord for production	
	2	Landlord for furnish	
	3	Landlord for production and furnish	
	4	Landlord for production, merchant for furnish	
	5	Landlord for furnish, merchant for production	
	6	Landlord for production, other source of furnish credit	
	7	Landlord for furnish, other source of production	
	8	Other types of credit guaranteed by landlord	
	9	Other types of credit not guaranteed by landlord	
	X	Other types of credit with landlord waiver of rent	
	Y	Credit—source N.A.	

36		Housing, *socio-economic status*	*Section C
	1	36-39	
	2	40-44	
	3	45-49	
	4	50-54	
	5	55-59	
	6	60-64	
	7	65-69	
	8	70-74	
	9	75-78	

Column Number	Code and Item		Location on Schedule
37		Crop *yield* index	*Section D
	0	0.00- .29	
	1	.30- .49	
	2	.50- .69	
	3	.70- .89	
	4	.90-1.09	
	5	1.10-1.29	
	6	1.30-1.49	
	7	1.50-1.69	
	8	1.70-1.89	
	9	1.90-2.09	
	X	2.10 and over	
	Y	N.A.	
38		Head or spouse, highest *education* of	Section B, line 1, 2 column (1)
	0	No education	
	1	Grades 1 and 2	
	2	Grades 3 and 4	
	3	Grades 5 and 6	
	4	Grades 7 and 8	
	5	High school 1 or 2	
	6	High school 3 or 4	
	7	College 1 or 2	
	8	College 3 or 4	
	Y	N.A.	
39		Rent tract, years on *(moves)*	Section K
	1	1	
	2	2	
	3	3	
	4	4	
	5	5-9	
	6	10-14	
	7	15-19	
	8	20-24	
	9	25 and over	
	Y	N.A.	
40		Age of *landlord*	Section F, Item4c
	1	20-	
	2	30-	
	3	40-	
	4	50-	
	5	60-	
	6	70-	
	7	80-	
	8	90 and over	
	X	(Estate or Institution)	
	Y	N.A.	

SAMPLE OF EXPLANATION OF CODES. These definitions and explanations were worked out in a general way during the formulation of the schedules but were extensively revised and added to during the tabulation and analysis of the data. This work was coordinated through the Regional Office by means of a 5 x 8 card system. Each tenure worker in the region was a cooperator in this work and was furnished a complete file of the definitions together with the various changes as the work progressed. Necessary changes in old definitions and additions of new ones were accomplished by adjusting the card files accordingly. By the time all codes had been sent out the *Explanation of Codes* file contained a total of 42 guide cards (major subject matter headings) and 344 subject matter cards. The definitions were not officially adopted for project use until passed on by all workers concerned. During the course of the study it was discovered that there existed within the region a considerable diversity in the use of terms. Regional clearance in the use of these terms is considered to have been one of the important advantages of the regional cooperative research approach. In the past, valid comparison of state data has been greatly handicapped. In many instances comparisons have not been attempted in the face of variations in definitions; in other instances researchers have made spurious comparisons due to differences in the usage of terms of which they were unaware. The accompanying sample constitutes the materials on the 12 subject matter cards filed under the guide card, *Moves.*

MOVES

Increase in total acres of present farm over previous farm. This applies to the situation immediately preceding and following the last move and not to change in size of farm apart from moving.

Last move of family. The code is based on a logarithmic series of mile intervals, on the assumption that distance is thus related to factors that induce migration.

Migration index. The average number of moves previously made by each "five years of earning life" group of farm family heads was used to produce a generalized smooth curve. (For further explanation see Editing Procedure, The Migration Index.)

Miles from home. The distance of the child's residence from its parents' present residence measured in miles. The intervals of miles distance are logarithmic series. This has been termed the radius of migration from the parental home.

Moves with no change in school, church or trade center. A change in church, school and trade center is deemed to represent a change in neighborhood. For the Arkansas sample these data were obtained for the years 1932 to 1942 only. From these measures and total number of moves the number of moves within the neighborhood area and between such areas was measured.

Number of moves. This constituted a simple count of all entries other than zero for miles moved. Unless there were schedule notes to the contrary an entry of zero for miles moved and a non-farm occupation was considered as one move to a new location and an additional move to the next farm.

Place of birth and first tenure/occupational experience. Since the sample areas in Arkansas and Mississippi were adjacent to the state of Louisiana, an additional category was set up for Louisiana as a place of birth for those cases sampled in Arkansas and Mississippi. Southern States included all the states in the Regional Project and extended north to the Ohio River and east to the Atlantic. West Virginia was not classified as a Southern State but Virginia was. Midwestern States began with Ohio and included all states to the west as far as the Kansas, Nebraska, Dakota tier of states including Missouri. "Other states" were New Mexico, Colorado, Washington, and Oregon. The foreign countries represented in place of birth were Czechoslovakia-15, Germany and Mexico—3 each; and one case each from England, Russia, Sweden and Austria-Hungary.

Range of child's residence. The present residence of the child away from the parental home was measured by categories of political boundaries—county and state. (Note that only the present residence of parents and of child is considered.)

Residence by census classification. The present residence of the child away from home was classified as farm, rural-nonfarm, urban or other. Other includes rural when not designated as farm or non-farm. It also includes urban area, when not designated as whether inside or outside the corporate limits.

Type of moves and distance. Each case was classified as belonging to one of three types of moves or combinations of these types. The points selected for breaking the class intervals were the same points as used for other measures of distance moved and were the troughs of the frequency distribution curve for distance moved. The three distances approximate intra-neighborhood moves, intra-county moves and inter-county moves. Classification is based on reported changes. If the distance of all moves was not reported, consideration was given to place of birth and visiting with neighbors who were related to determine the classification.

Years on this farm. This refers to consecutive years the cooperator operated or worked for wages on this farm. If the cooperator rented out the entire farm, such renting out would break the continuity of "years on this farm."

Years on this farm is a measure of stability on the present operating unit as either owner, part owner, renter, cropper, or wage hand. It coincides with the term as used by the census excepting that wage labor has been added. Unless there was information to the contrary, schedule entries other than zero for miles moved were taken to indicate a change in farm.

Years on rent tract. Number of consecutive years, including 1942, the operator operated all or part of the rent tract under consideration.

SAMPLE SHOWING METHOD OF TRANSMITTAL OF STA-
TISTICAL REPORTS TO THE STATES. The statistical reports as elsewhere indicated were run on a 405 Hollerith Accounting Machine. All
reports were printed by the machine in duplicate and in some instances in
triplicate so that a copy could be retained in the Regional Office and one
or more identical copies sent to the state concerned. Each state normally
received only its own statistical reports. A total of 2819 statistical reports
were sent to the five states, or an average of over 560 to each state. Later
in the project the regional staff, for purposes of regional analysis, put
together in table form various phases of the statistical reports from all the
states. In other words, regional tables were constructed. These regional
tables were sent to all of the states so that each state worker had the advantage of comparing identical materials from the other states with his
own. A total of 273 such tables were compiled in the Regional Office and
sent to each of the states.

The following memorandum of transmittal from the Regional Office
together with a description of the statistical reports which were enclosed
shows how the data were sent to the states. A sample of an actual statistical report is not included since they are entirely in code numbers. With
the code book however they were readily worked into standard statistical
tables. In addition, the material as presented in the statistical reports gave
considerable leeway as to the use to which it could be put in the several
states.

It will be noted in the accompanying covering memorandum that
although in this instance comparable materials are sent to the several
states some exceptions are made because of state differences. Also, in this
particular shipment of data, only four of the five states are included, the
other one not having comparable data for the items in question.

Appendix 4

Regional Land Tenure Research Project
213 North Church Street
Fayetteville, Arkansas

September 15, 1945

MEMORANDUM

To: Osgood (Arkansas)
       Todd (Mississippi)
       Davis (Oklahoma)
       McMillan (Oklahoma)
       Allen (Texas)

From: Harold Hoffsommer, Director, Regional Land Tenure
       Research Project

Subject: Transmittal of Statistical Reports for Cards 7, A and 9.

Enclosed herewith are the following seventy-four (74) (71 for Texas) Statistical Reports as described on the attached pages:

       Card 7—Reports 1 to 44 inclusive
       Card A—Reports 1 to 27 inclusive
       Card 9—Reports 1 to 3 inclusive (excepting Texas)

The three Card 9 reports are not available for Texas since they involve net income and expense items not secured for individual farms in that state.

Copies to: Ackerman
           Charlton
           Magee
           Miley

REPORTS

Case count of leases with sorts by crop method of rental payment (24) and by color and national origin (3) (except Oklahoma) showing frequency distributions by items as follows:

7 - 1   Present tenure status of head (4).
7 - 2   Type of farming (9).
7 - 3   Socio-economic status scale (10).
7 - 4   Migration index (11).
7 - 5   Diversification index (21).
7 - 6   Type of lease—form and length (22).
7 - 7   Property covered by lease (23).
7 - 8   Livestock method of rental payment (25).
7 - 9   Ratio of rental payment to farm business rented (26)
7-10   Wages from landlord, per cent of gross income (27).
7-11   Color and sex of landlord (28).
7-12   Occupation of landlord (29).
7-13   Kinship to landlord (30).
7-14   Distance from farm to residence of landlord (31).
7-15   Frequency of supervision by landlord (32).
7-16   Rent tract index of management (33).
7-17   Number of families supervised by landlord (34).
7-18   Source of production and furnish credit (35).
7-19   Crop yield index (37).
7-20   Highest education of head or spouse (38).
7-21   Years on rent tract (39).
7-22   Age of landlord (40).
7-23   Division of cotton seed expense (44).
7-24   Division of cotton fertilizer expense (45).
7-25   Division of harvesting expense (46).
7-26   Division of ginning expense (47).
7-27   Division of spray material expense (48).
7-28   Division of hauling expense for cash crops (49).
7-29   Division of processing expense (other than ginning) (50).
7-30   Division of machine hire expense (51).
7-31   Division of repair cost for materials for dwelling (52).
7-32   Division of repair cost for materials for "other" (53).
7-33   Division of hauling expense for cotton (54).
7-34   Division of unpaid labor or improvement repair (55).
7-35   Division of cotton lint production (56).
7-36   Division of cottonseed production (57).
7-37   Division of feed crop production (58).
7-38   Division of other cash crop production (59).
7-39   Division of peanut production (60).
7-40   Division of alfalfa seed production (61).
7-41   Division of alfalfa hay production (62).
7-42   Division of AAA payments (63).
7-43   Delivery of feed crop rent (division) (76).
7-44   Number of lease (77).

REPORTS

Case count of families and tabulation of items with sorts by present tenure status of head (4) and color and national origin (3) showing frequency distributions and totals by items as follows:

A - 1 Tabulation of: age of head (22-23); number of moves since first year of earning life (45-46); years on this farm (53-54); years as owner (55-56); years as renter (57-58) with sorts as outlined above.

A - 2 Tabulation of: years as cropper (59-60); years as farm laborer (61-62); years in non-farm occupation (63-64); years of earning life (65-66); and increase in total acres of present farm over previous farm (69-70-71) with sorts as outlined above.

A - 3 Kinship to landlord (25) (Code X ignored).
A - 4 Age at beginning of earning life (27).
A - 5 Type of tenure change (28) (Code X ignored).
A - 6 Grade retardation of children in school (33).
A - 7 Grade retardation of children completed school (34).
A - 8 Room—person ration (35).
A - 9 Man equivalent units of family labor available (36).
A-10 Fertility index (37).
A-11 Participation in public work relief programs (38).
A-12 Credit used, per cent of farm business owned (39).
A-13 Place of birth (41).
A-14 Place of first tenure/occupational experience (42).
A-15 Type of move—distance (43).
A-16 Moves with no tenure change (47).
A-17 Tenure change up with no move (48).
A-18 Tenure change down with no move (49).
A-19 Moves with no change in school (50).
A-20 Moves with no change in church (51).
A-21 Moves with no change in trade center (52).
A-22 Number of moves 0.62 miles or less (72).
A-23 Number of moves 0.63 to 3.9 miles (73).
A-24 Number of moves 4.0 to 9.9 miles (74).
A-25 Number of moves 10.0 to 24.9 miles (75).
A-26 Number of moves 25.0 to 158.9 miles (76).
A-27 Number of moves 159.0 miles and over (77).

REPORTS

Case count and tabulation of farms for Arkansas, Mississippi and Oklahoma with sorts by color and national origin (3), acres in cropland (5) and present tenure status of head (4). All cases of N.A. for operator's earning (69-70-71-72) (Y in 72), and tenures of indeterminate, laborer and "other" (Codes 3, 9 and 0 in Col. 4) were discarded.

Arkansas—The regular sample was considered. The cards were grouped by acres of cropland (5) into groups of under 40 acres, 40 to 59.9 acres and 60 acres and over. Part owners (Code 2 in Col. 4) and other tenant (Code 8 in Col. 4) were discarded. Cash tenants (Code 4 in Col. 4) and share-cash tenants (Code 6 in Col. 4) were combined.

Mississippi—Cash tenants, share-cash tenants, share tenants and other tenants (Codes of 4, 5, 6 and 8 in Col. 4) were combined into one group. The cards were grouped by acres of cropland (5) into groups of under 20 acres, 20 to 39.9 acres, 40 to 79.9 acres, and 80 acres and over. The cards were further sorted into two major groups of those using cropper labor and those not using cropper labor.

Oklahoma—No sort was made on color and national origin (3) for Oklahoma. The other sorting factors used the full code as indicated.

9 - 1   Tabulation of gross farm income (17 to 20); feed purchased or feed purchased and crop expenses (21 to 23); fertilizer purchased or livestock expenses (24 to 26); taxes paid (27 to 29); machinery operation and repairs (30 to 32) cost of hired labor (33 to 36); cost of cropper labor (37 to 40) with sorts as outlined above.

9 - 2   Tabulation of real estate repairs or building depreciation (41 to 43); interest on production credit (44-45); interest on real estate credit or workstock depreciation or value of operator's labor (46 to 48); cash rent paid (49 to 51); cash value of share rental payment (52 to 55); miscellaneous farm expense (56 to 58) and interest on investment (59 to 61) with sorts as outlined above.

9 - 3   Tabulation of family earnings (62 to 65); value of unpaid family labor (66 to 68); operator's earnings (69 to 72); other income (73 to 75); net family income (76-77) with sorts as outlined above.

SAMPLE REGIONAL TABLE. Two hundred and seventy-three such tables were compiled in the Regional Office incident to analysing the regional materials. A copy of each was sent to each of the states. These copies were sent out, however, considerably later than the statistical reports. In the numerical designation 6:1b the "6" indicates that the materials came largely from Card 6. "1b" indicates the number of this particular table in the Card 6 series.

Table 6:1b. Characteristics of leasee by length and type of leasing arrangement for 1037 leases in four sample areas of the South Central Region.

Area and type of lease	Number of leases	Average value for specified items			
		Migration index[1]	Years of earning life	Division of management[2]	Diversification index[3]
Arkansas Coastal Plain					
Oral, indefinite	82	94	28	75	2.98
Oral, 1 year	251	112	23	65	3.21
Written, 1 year	90	124	25	84	3.32
Written, 2 years and over	30	113	26	87	3.36
Mississippi Coastal Plain					
Oral, indefinite	27	89	17	52	3.14
Oral, 1 year	131	121	21	42	2.96
Written, 1 year	9	126	23	78	3.03
Written, 2 years and over	10	93	29	85	3.48
Oklahoma Rolling Plain					
Oral, indefinite	68	80	21	82	3.28
Oral, 1 year	84	118	24	75	3.20
Written, 1 year	38	108	22	79	3.18
Written, 2 years and over	24	142	25	79	3.54
Texas Blackland Prairie					
Oral, indefinite	52	68	20	82	3.28
Oral, 1 year	174	83	20	82	3.28
Written, 1 year	42	79	23	78	3.13
Written, 2 years and over	8	81	21	79	3.38

1. Region migration ratio is .6709 and equals base of 100.

2. High score indicates a high proportion of the managing done by the leasee.

3. Increase in numerical value indicates more diversification.

MATERIALS DEVELOPED IN CONNECTION WITH THE REGIONAL
LAND TENURE RESEARCH PROJECT

ARKANSAS

Bulletins

1945 Aug.—Land Tenure in Arkansas. IV Further Changes in Labor Used on Cotton Farms, 1939-44. Otis T. Osgood and John W. White. Arkansas Agricultural Experiment Station. Fayetteville. Bulletin 459.

1947 June—The Legal Aspects of Farm Tenancy in Arkansas. Erling D. Solberg. Arkansas Agricultural Experiment Station. Fayetteville. Bulletin 468.

1947 Sept.—Social Aspects of Farm Ownership and Tenancy in the Arkansas Ozarks. J. L. Charlton. Arkansas Agricultural Experiment Station. Fayetteville. Bulletin 471.

1947 Dec.—The Organization and Income on Owner and Tenant Farms in Boone County. Melvin W. Slusher and Otis T. Osgood. Arkansas Agricultural Experiment Station. Fayetteville. Bulletin 472.

(In Preparation)

The Social Aspects of Land Tenure in the Arkansas Coastal Plains. Health and Medical Care as Related to Tenure Status and Other Factors.

Farm Organization and Income Data for Arkansas Coastal Plains.

Thesis

1947—Analyzing Farm Organization and Income for Arkansas Coastal Plains. D. A. Marshall. (Doctoral thesis)

LOUISIANA

Bulletins

1945 Aug.—Farm Ownership in Louisiana Financed Under the Bank-head-Jones Farm Tenant Act. Willie Mae Alexander. Louisiana Agricultural Experiment Station. Baton Rouge. Bulletin 397.

Journal Article

1945 May—"Acquiring Farm Ownership in Louisiana Under the Bank-head-Jones Farm Tenant Act." Willie Mae Alexander. *Louisiana Rural Economist*, Vol. 7, No. 2, p. 3.

Thesis

1943—Farm Tenure Conditions in the Hilly Area of Lincoln Parish, Louisiana. Louis F. Moore. (Master's thesis)

MISSISSIPPI

Bulletins

1944 June—Organization and Operation of Farms in Black Prairie Area, Mississippi. W. G. O'Leary. Mississippi Agricultural Experiment Station. State College. Bulletin 404.

1946 June—Some Implications of Land Tenure in the Longleaf Pine Area of Mississippi. D. Gray Miley. Mississippi Agricultural Experiment Station. State College. Bulletin 430.

Journal Article

1945 July—"Productivity and Income by Tenure Groups, 310 Farms." H. P. Todd. *Mississippi Farm Research*. Mississippi Agricultural Experiment Station. State College. Vol. 8, No. 7, p. 7.

OKLAHOMA

Bulletins

1945 Oct.—Social Factors Related to Farm Housing in Southern Oklahoma. Robert T. McMillan. Oklahoma Agricultural Experiment Station. Stillwater. Technical Bulletin T-22.

1945 Nov.—Social Factors of Farm Ownership in Oklahoma. Robert T. McMillan and Otis Durant Duncan. Oklahoma Agricultural Experiment Station. Stillwater. Bulletin 289.

1945 Nov.—Farm Housing in Southern Oklahoma. Robert T. McMillan. Oklahoma Agricultural Experiment Station. Stillwater. Bulletin 290.

(In Preparation)

Social Selection Among Children of Rural Families.

Journal Articles

1943 Nov.—"Hypotheses in Land Tenure Research." Otis Durant Duncan. *Journal of Farm Economics*, Vol. XXV, No. 4, pp. 860-68.

1944 Oct.—" 'Absentee' Landlords." Randall T. Klemme. *Current Farm Economics*. Oklahoma Agricultural Experiment Station and Department of Agricultural Economics. Stillwater. Vol. 17, No. 5, pp. 137-43.

1945 Oct.—"Some Observations on Farm Ownership in Southeastern Oklahoma." Robert T. McMillan. *Current Farm Economics*. Oklahoma Agricultural Experiment Station and Department of Agricultural Economics. Stillwater. Vol. 18, No. 5, pp. 106-10.

1945 Dec.—"Social Backgrounds and Farm Ownership." Robert T. McMillan and Marylee Mason. *Rural Sociology*, Vol. 10, No. 4 (Dec. 1945), pp. 414-16.

1945 Dec.—"Land Tenure and Pasture Conservation." Peter Nelson. *Current Farm Economics*. Oklahoma Agricultural Experiment Station and Department of Agricultural Economics. Stillwater. Vol. 18, No. 6, pp. 141-45.

1946—"The Influence of Fathers and Mothers Upon the Social Traits of Children." Robert T. McMillan. *Southwestern Journal*, Vol. 2, No. 3, pp. 211-19.

1946 Oct.—"School Acceleration and Retardation Among Village Children in Southern Oklahoma." Robert T. McMillan. *Journal of Educational Research*, Vol. XL, No. 2, pp. 126-32.

1946 Nov.—"Are Tenure Differences Due to Tenure?" Robert T. McMillan. *Journal of Farm Economics*, Vol. XXVIII, No. 4, pp. 1029-36.

1946 Dec.—"School Acceleration and Retardation Among Open Country Children in Southern Oklahoma." Robert T. McMillan. *Rural Sociology*, Vol. 11, No. 4, pp. 339-45.

Mimeographed Report

1944 Oct.—Farm Tenancy Areas in Oklahoma. John Hoyle Southern. United States Department of Agriculture, Bureau of Agricultural Economics in cooperation with Oklahoma Agricultural Experiment Station. Little Rock, Arkansas.

TEXAS

Bulletins

1944 June—Recent Trend in Land Tenure in Texas. Joe R. Motheral. Texas Agricultural Experiment Station. College Station. Bulletin 641.

1947 April—The Price of Texas Farm and Ranch Lands, 1920-1945. Joe R. Motheral. Texas Agricultural Experiment Station. College Station. Bulletin 688.

(In Preparation)

Legal Aspects of Farm Tenancy in Texas.

Farm Leases in the Texas Black Prairie.

Journal Articles

1943 Aug.—"Here We Go Again." *Farm and Ranch*. Joe R. Motheral.

1946—"Observations Among the Czechoslovaks in Eastern Bell County, Texas." Sandor B. Kovacs. *Southwestern Journal*, Vol. 2, No. 4, pp. 293-95.

1947—"Notice of Termination—A Farm Lease Problem in Texas." Joe R. Motheral. *Southwestern Social Science Quarterly*, Vol. XXVIII, No. 1, pp. 20-35.

Mimeographed Reports

1943 Oct.—Use of Labor by Farm Operators of Different Tenure Status in the Texas Black Prairie. Joe R. Motheral. Texas Agricultural Experiment Station. College Station. Progress Report No. 862.

1945 Nov.—Trend in the Sales Price of Farm and Ranch Lands in Texas, 1920-1944. L. P. Gabbard, Erwin C. Ford, and J. Lambert Molyneaux. Texas Agricultural Experiment Station. College Station. Progress Report No. 971.

Thesis

1947—An Analysis of the Influence of Social Factors on Farm Income in Eastern Bell County, Texas. Robert L. Skrabanek. (Master's thesis)

REGIONAL

Journal Articles

1943 Feb.—"Organization and Objectives of the Regional Land Tenure Research Project." Harold Hoffsommer. *Journal of Farm Economics,* Vol. XXV, No. 1, pp. 245-57.

1947—"Some Tenure Implications of Wartime Land Transfers in the Southwest." John Hoyle Southern. *Southwestern Social Science Quarterly,* Vol. XXVIII, No. 2, pp. 145-54.

Book

The Social and Economic Significance of Land Tenure in the Southwestern States. Harold Hoffsommer (Ed.) University of North Carolina Press, Chapel Hill, N. C. (In process of publication.) See also pre-print of the summary chapter of this book, published under the title "Land Tenure in the Southwestern States," Southwestern Regional Bulletin No. 1, Arkansas Agricultural Experiment Station Bulletin No. 482, Fayetteville, October, 1948.

www.ingramcontent.com/pod-product-compliance
Lightning Source LLC
Chambersburg PA
CBHW021601210326
41599CB00010B/551